Teaching in the Digital Age
for Preschool and Kindergarten

Other Redleaf Press Books by Brian Puerling

Teaching in the Digital Age: Smart Tools for Age 3 to Grade 3
Teaching in the Digital Age: PowerPoint Presentations (CD-ROM)
Children in the Digital Age: A Guide for Families

Teaching
IN THE
Digital Age
for Preschool and Kindergarten

**Enhancing Curriculum
with Technology**

Brian Puerling

Redleaf Press®
www.redleafpress.org
800-423-8309

Published by Redleaf Press
10 Yorkton Court
St. Paul, MN 55117
www.redleafpress.org

First edition 2018
Cover design by Jim Handrigan
Cover photographs by iStock.com/Asergieiev and Jim Handrigan
Interior design by Jim Handrigan
Typeset in Minion Pro
Interior photos by David Recksieck
Printed in the United States of America
24 23 22 21 20 19 18 17   1 2 3 4 5 6 7 8

This book contains names of numerous products and the companies that produce them. Neither the author nor Redleaf Press endorse or sell any of the products mentioned and is not affiliated with any of the businesses that produce them. Redleaf Press is not responsible for any dissatisfaction you may experience with any of the products or businesses referred to herein.

Library of Congress Cataloging-in-Publication Data
    Names: Puerling, Brian, author.
    Title: Teaching in the digital age for preschool and kindergarten : enriching
        curriculum with technology / Brian Puerling.
    Description: St. Paul, MN : Redleaf Press, [2018] | Includes bibliographical
        references and index.
    Identifiers: LCCN 2017031654 (print) | LCCN 2017049849 (ebook) | ISBN
        9781605546025 (e-book) | ISBN 9781605542942 (pbk. : acid-free paper)
    Subjects: LCSH: Education, Preschool--Computer-assisted instruction. |
        Education, Preschool--Curricula. | Education--Effect of technological
        innovations on. | Educational technology.
    Classification: LCC LB1140.35.C64 (ebook) | LCC LB1140.35.C64 P84 2018
        (print) | DDC 372.21--dc23
    LC record available at https://lccn.loc.gov/2017031654

Printed on acid-free paper

To my daughter, Lydia Joy

Contents

Foreword

As Executive Director of the Fred Rogers Center, I have the good fortune to work with leading experts at the crossroads of child development, technology, and education. Given the rapidly changing technology landscape, using digital media and technology to support the social-emotional well-being and cognitive skills of children is vitally important. Just as Fred Rogers used television—the technology of his day—to inspire, nurture, and educate young children, today's technology has the potential to enrich learning.

Recently, we released a new report in collaboration with TEC Center at Erikson Institute, *Technology and Interactive Media for Young Children: A Whole Child Approach Connecting the Vision of Fred Rogers with Research and Practice.* The report highlighted that media, technology, and social-emotional development are not mutually exclusive and that there is considerable room for growth in how media and technology is designed and utilized to support whole child development. For many, including myself, translating this into practice is often challenging.

So, when Fred Rogers Center Early Career Fellow Brian Puerling asked me if I would consider writing the foreword to his latest book the answer was a quick yes. I first met Brian when I joined the Fred Rogers Center in 2014, and through the years we have connected at conferences and professional development conventions. But it wasn't until I visited Brian at Chicago's Catherine Cook School that I fully appreciated his natural talent for taking technology and translating it into practice that is mindful of children's social-emotional development and cognitive skills.

As we walked around the school, I had the opportunity to witness how he integrated technology in the teaching environment. It was clear that Brian had a special gift. The way the children and their teachers used technology was seamless—it wasn't using technology for technology's sake. In one classroom, I watched as children and teachers engaged with one another as they were creating a stop-motion video. The collaboration and persistence skills the children were learning will serve them well throughout their lives. Technology didn't get in the way—it enhanced their interactions and promoted deeper learning.

As I finished my tour with Brian, I was both impressed and saddened. Impressed because I had just experienced what many of us have envisioned as the potential for technology to transform the classroom. Then it hit me, even if schools had all the technologies at their disposal, they still don't have the luxury of a dedicated person such as Brian to help develop curriculum and work side by side with teachers to support professional development and best practices.

That's why I was thrilled when Brian told me about his new book, which allows him to bring his years of experience and finely-honed practices to a wider audience. His straightforward examples in each subject area allow educators to quickly connect the dots and then apply that knowledge to any new technology that may come their way in a wide variety of subjects. Brian's background in child development truly shines through in his approach.

While there are many respected books, surveys, reports, and positions statements on the topic of technology use in the classroom, such as the joint position statement by the National Association of Education of Young Children and Fred Rogers Center, they always encourage using technology in alignment with child development practices, but they rarely say how. In this book, Brian clearly states numerous practical examples on how technology can be used to expand children's learning and encourages teachers to build on what they already know about pedagogy.

In chapter seven, Brian tells the story of a current student who was moving away with her family. Because she was aware of some of the ways in which people can keep in touch, she chose to stay connected to her school and classroom through video messaging. This experience not only changed students understanding of geography, but enabled them to maintain a strong social connection.

In the same chapter, he goes through the process of creating a feelings book/e-reader and corresponding with digital pen pals. These are all opportunities that young children who wouldn't necessarily have the advanced writing skills, or emotional vocabulary to express themselves on paper, are now able to have. To quote Brian from the book, "Developing social-emotional skills does not only happen face to face. There are other ways children can connect and develop relationships with people while still in the classroom, in the home, on the playground, at the pool, and in the car."

To help teachers decide which social platforms to use for sharing information, Brian has seven questions that will guide making a selection. Brian says, "No matter what the experience is, it is important that teachers are well aware of the social-emotional state of the group and use that as the guide for the tools they decide to use with the group, rather than choosing a tool or resource first, and then finding a way to make it work for the social-emotional state of the group." Brian's gentle reminder to not forget about emotions—something all of us bring to learning—is something I will be quoting again and again.

Although *Teaching in the Digital Age for Preschool and Kindergarten* is intended for educators, it is incredibly helpful for parents as well. As the father of two amazing young daughters, I see how my children and their teachers use technology in the classroom and how technology integration continuously evolves. This book is a great resource as I think about my own technology interactions with my daughters and how it can enhance and strengthen our relationship as a family. Many of us are learning as quickly as we can when it comes to technology use with children, and this book can be our trusted companion in guiding us forward.

—Rick Fernandes

Acknowledgments

I want to extend my gratitude to several individuals at Catherine Cook School—Jean Robbins, Max Weinberg, Cory Stutts, Michael Roberts, Rachel Pujol, and Stacy Shafer Peterson for their ongoing support and encouragement in the process of developing this book. They have always been available for an impromptu drop-in from me for advice.

I would also like to recognize the tremendous and generous flexibility Redleaf has offered. David Heath and Kara Lomen have been extremely helpful along the way, and I am truly grateful. Danny Miller, my editor for this book, was a great collaborator; I appreciate his time and effort making this book what it has become.

Kyra Ostendorf was my editor for my first book and has ever since remained a good friend and colleague. I want to underscore how much I value her encouragement and support over the past several years.

I want to thank David Recksieck for his ongoing support and flexibility as this book was pulled together near the end. I truly appreciate his attention to detail and creative eye. His last-minute efforts were helpful more than he will ever know. High five and a hug!

I want to acknowledge all of those whom I mention or referred to in this book, as they have influenced me in some positive way as I developed the concept and approach for this book: Ashley Marentette, Laura Freidman, Peter Pizzolongo, Barb Gander, Barb Chaney, Rachel Hill, Amanda Burns, Barb Fisher, Lauren Goldberg, Amanda Beights, Michael Linn, Filippo Yacob, Elisa Gall, Sandra Kane, Jean Robbins, April Lutes, Kate Cherry, Sammi Littel, and Malcolm Scott.

My daughter, Lydia, has been a great help, as she has been my in-house laboratory with trying out applications, devices, and other resources. Her smile and positive attitude have always provided me with such encouragement. I also want to acknowledge her mom, Emily Gill, who was extremely supportive in the initial phases of this book. This book would not exist without her.

Introduction
Goals and Intentions of This Book

AT CATHERINE COOK SCHOOL, just north of downtown Chicago, where I am the director of education technology, we explore issues regarding technology and digital media with our students and families. We have an orientation that helps families understand how our program utilizes technology and digital media as a tool for learning. Parent-teacher conferences and informal conversations are also used to continue this discussion throughout the school year. Across the grade levels, we talk about the importance and value of sharing learning with other students and the community. This sharing can be done in a variety of ways: face-to-face at a school event, a newsletter (print or electronic), informal e-mails, video conferencing, videos, and podcasts are just a few examples, and that applies to preschool and kindergarten students as well.

Such sharing, of course, happens in all subject areas: science, mathematics, literacy, art, social studies, health, physical education, and music. We also discuss the reasons why we might share our learning. For example, students might share what they learned about African animals in an e-book to help others become more knowledgeable about the animals that live in other parts of the world. Students might share what they learned about an author during an author study by creating a book trailer video to help get other readers interested in that author's books. Students might e-mail their teachers an illustration they created in an iPad application so that the teachers can learn more about what they are able to draw and convey with artwork. These conversations and opportunities are important because we build on these conversations in the grades to come. For example, in first grade we talk about the purpose of the "cc" option in an e-mail. The following conversation occurred between me and a child:

> **Mr. Puerling**: Boys and girls, writers may use the "cc" option to keep other individuals in the conversation who might not necessarily need to be part of the conversation. For example, let's say that your teacher, Ms. Marentette, was planning a field trip to the zoo. If she was talking with the zoo staff using e-mail, she might "cc" the other two first-grade teachers so that they know what is going on as well. Ms. Marentette would be using the "cc" option to let the other teachers listen in on the conversation.

> **Victor** (first grade student): Mr. Puerling, so when I e-mail Ms. Marentette what I make on the iPad, can I "cc" Ms. Friedman (teaching assistant) so she knows what I am doing too?

> **Mr. Puerling**: Victor, that's a perfect example of when you, as a first grader, might use the "cc" option.

These conversations are crucial to help our students develop positive and responsible uses of technology and digital media (Levin 2013; Scheibe and Rogow 2012). They are a part of our school community just as much as our conversations regarding bullying and character development are.

In 2012, Lisa Guernsey, Michael Levine, Cynthia Chiong, and Maggie Severns published an article, *Pioneering Literacy in the Digital Wild West: Empowering Parents and Educators*, which highlighted the immediate needs for further growth in the developmentally appropriate integration of technology and digital media to support skill development in areas such as literacy:

- Publish guidelines on choosing digital media, encouraging parents [and educators] to use media to learn together with children.

- Train teachers how to integrate technology into reading instruction when appropriate.

- Expand media literacy curricula to include preschool and primary grades.

Teachers need time to explore and discover new strategies (Jackson 2013). They also need time to reflect and think about how these strategies can be used in their classrooms with their groups. This book, *Teaching in the Digital Age for Preschool and Kindergarten: Enhancing Curriculum with Technology*, is intended to address these very needs.

In 2012, I came out with *Teaching in the Digital Age: Smart Tools for Age 3 to Grade 3*. That book provided tips and tools for developmentally appropriate technology and digital media integration. It provided readers with ideas and vignettes of how teachers have used technology and digital media to support children's identity as authors, illustrators, artists, musicians, researchers, mathematicians, and scientists. QR codes were linked to videos of classroom strategies in action and teachers reflecting on techniques they have tried. This book is intended to build on the ideas and approaches in that book and dig deeper into the goals and subject areas of preschool and kindergarten children. Additionally, the strategies provided in this book build the idea of helping children develop an identity in the roles listed above and expand into other roles, including veterinarians, programmers, meteorologists, videographers, recording/remixing artists, animators, filmmakers, and designers.

In Diane Levin's book *Beyond Remote-Controlled Childhood: Teaching Young Children in the Media Age*, she describes concerns regarding the presence of certain media in the lives of young children. Levin aimed to provide a resource to help teachers and parents make conscious decisions about when, how, and why they use media with young children. With this book, I hope to do the same with technology and media in the classroom context. My hope is that this book, as Levin stated in her book, "will help you take action . . . to move beyond the negatives and promote the positives for all children" (2013, 19).

How This Book Is Organized

The first chapter of this book addresses two key points: the importance of professional development and the obstacles related to implementing strategies learned in professional development experiences. These obstacles are important to consider when implementing any new classroom practice. After acknowledging these obstacles, the chapter moves into the second key point, which is reminding readers of the importance of adhering to an integrated curriculum approach. This reminder is crucial as each of the chapters that follow focuses on an individual subject area explored in early childhood classrooms: science, mathematics, literacy, art, music, social studies, health, and physical education. Because the book is structured in this way, it is important that teachers remain cognizant of planning with an integrated curriculum approach while trying out the ideas in this book.

Readers familiar with the structure of *Teaching in the Digital Age: Smart Tools for Age 3 to Grade 3* will recall that each chapter was divided into three sections: how the technology or media can support learning, support the ability to share learning, and support the ability to exhibit learning. The strategies in this book are discussed with two significant considerations: the NAEYC/Fred Rogers Center position statement called *Technology and Interactive Media as Tools in Early Childhood Programs Serving Children from Birth through Age 8* (2012) and the TPACK model (which stands for Technological Pedagogical and Content Knowledge), developed by Dr. Matthew Koehler. The NAEYC/FRC position statement is intended to provide teachers with the theoretical approach to thinking and planning with child development, research, technology, and digital media in mind. At a session lead by Chip Donohue at a recent NAEYC Conference, Peter Pizzolongo made an important point: the position statement is an approach to thinking and planning. The "how to," on the other hand, comes from books such as this and others, including the following:

- *Digital Decisions: Choosing the Right Technology Tools for Early Childhood Education* (Simon and Nemeth 2012)

- *Instructional Technology in Early Childhood* (Parette and Blum 2013)

- *Invent to Learn: Making, Tinkering, and Engineering in the Classroom* (Libow Martinez and Stager 2013)

- *Spotlight on Young Children and Technology* (Shillady and Schoenberg Muccio 2012)

- *Teaching in the Digital Age: Smart Tools for Age 3 to Grade 3* (Puerling 2012)

- *Technology and Digital Media in the Early Years: Tools for Teaching and Learning* (Donohue 2014)

The TPACK model reminds teachers to consider three important elements in their technology and media integration:

- technical knowledge

- pedagogical knowledge

- content knowledge

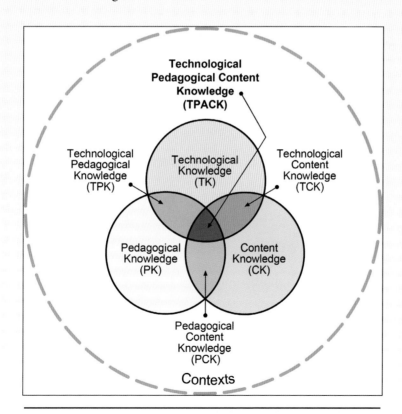

http://tpack.org. Photo reproduced by permission of the publisher, © 2012 by tpack.org.

Pedagogical knowledge refers to a teacher's consideration of education theory and child development in planning and teaching. Technological knowledge refers to a teacher's skill set and ability to use technology as a tool for teaching and learning. Content knowledge refers to a teacher's ideas regarding the scope and sequence of knowledge, skills, and dispositions in each of the subject areas across grade levels: for example, knowing that preschool children learn to appreciate themselves and their family members before learning to appreciate others and their families. These areas of knowledge are essential in achieving the most intentional and authentic integration of technology and digital media.

Additional considerations in describing the strategies throughout this book can be summarized by Carrice Cummins, president of the International Reading Association. In the IRA journal, *Reading Today*, she published an article, "Celebrating Teachers: Using Technology to Make a Difference" (2013), which highlighted quick ideas to consider when implementing technology and digital media:

- Technology should be in the hands of students.

- Children do not have to know everything about the technology to begin using it.

- Technology is not just children in front of computers.

- Technology opens doors to expanded learning.

- Technology can be a motivational tool.

- Children, not the technology, are responsible for development.

This book includes QR codes to provide readers with the opportunity to learn more about various applications or resources. By scanning these QR codes using apps on their mobile devices, readers will be taken to links where they can learn more about the specific application, and can purchase and install it if they so choose. The mention of specific applications is not meant as an endorsement of these applications—there may very well be similar applications or resources available that are not mentioned in this book. Readers are encouraged to use their own judgment in choosing the best applications and resources for their particular classroom or site.

How to Use This Book

Readers should consider this a book of resources. As with *Teaching in the Digital Age: Smart Tools for Age 3 to Grade 3*, reading the book from beginning to end is not necessary. I recommend, however, that readers begin with chapter 1 and then move to a subject area of their choosing. My first book advocated for readers to identify a comfortable starting place in terms of technology integration. Identify your starting place by considering these issues:

- your own comfort level with trying new things

- your comfort level with technology

- technology strategies you've already tried

- the abilities/ages/development/background knowledge of the children in your class/group

- available resources (financial, administrative, parent, community, personnel)

- your own content area knowledge and expertise

How should you best proceed through this book? Consider the following examples:

READER 1: Mr. Silverstein

DESCRIPTION: Mr. Silverstein is a preschool teacher with a class of fifteen three-, four-, and five-year-old children. He has one teacher assistant. The families of the children in his classroom are very supportive of him integrating technology in his classroom. Mr. Silverstein is comfortable trying new things in his classroom. He feels confident teaching mathematics but feels like he has areas of improvement with teaching early literacy.

HOW MR. SILVERSTEIN CAN USE THIS BOOK: He begins reading chapter 1 and is reminded that if he is going to focus on an area of opportunity in his teaching that he cannot lose focus of the other important classroom experiences that require planning. He then moves on to chapter 4, which explores how to integrate technology in early literacy experiences. After reading this chapter, he gets a few ideas that he can try with the resources he has available to him. He begins with his five classroom iPads to introduce the idea of enjoying familiar books with an enhanced e-book experience.

READER 2: Ms. Goel

DESCRIPTION: Ms. Goel is a kindergarten teacher with thirty students and no classroom assistant. Her families are generally supportive of her using technology in the classroom, but at times she receives comments from some families wondering if she was using technology to simply entertain the class while she worked with other children. Ms. Goel is open to trying new things in her classroom but gets frustrated with where to start, given the lack of support she has.

HOW MS. GOEL CAN USE THIS BOOK: After reading chapter 1, she moves to chapter 7, which explores social studies. She is interested in determining how she can involve her families in the classroom and also show them how she is using technology in ways that are exciting, intentional, and rooted in curriculum. She learns about the idea of a secret e-reader. (An e-reader, in the context of this book, is an individual who shares a read-aloud with a group of students remotely using video conferencing software or applications.) She reaches out to a few parents with relatives who live in other states. After some conversation, she finds three family members who live out of state and who are interested in using Skype to read a story virtually to the class. Ms. Goel invites family members to come and be part of the surprise e-reader experience. After three secret e-reader events, she receives a few comments from some parents, acknowledging how nice it was to be able to bring those family members into the classroom virtually and how much the children enjoyed the experience.

My hope is that each teacher or administrator will use this book differently and in a way that best suits his needs. Good luck on your journey of trying new things and providing new experiences!

•   •   •

MEDIA CONSENT

Many of the strategies provided in this book direct you to take photographs and videos of children. In several cases, these strategies include ways to share the photographs and videos with others. Before you share photographs or videos of children, consult with your administrator to ensure that all necessary media consent forms are on file for the children. If consent forms are not on file, ask your administrator to provide one for you to have families sign. Explain to families how you plan to use photographs and videos. Be sure to include how you may use them to share how and what children have learned. The administration should keep signed consent forms on file each year from participating families.

An Integrated Approach to Curriculum

1

EARLY CHILDHOOD EDUCATORS ARE ALWAYS LOOKING for the best way to introduce new skills and concepts to children. In the field of education today, there are all sorts of ways to learn new strategies and remain aware of the most recent trends in education. Teachers read books, talk to other teachers, attend conferences, take classes, attend webinars, read blogs, and utilize social media platforms such as Facebook, Pinterest, and Twitter.

As teachers pick and choose the best ways to gather information in regard to their teaching, they establish a personalized Professional Learning Network (PLN). For example, if I were to describe my PLN, I would discuss how I use Twitter to get

Teachers can participate in online weekly Twitter chats. A few popular early childhood Twitter chats include #ecetechchat, #kinderchat, #1stchat, and #TeacherFriends. In these chats, teachers have access to all sorts of new ideas and resources.

a quick answer to a question; I read printed, bound professional texts so that I can leave notes in my margins and place sticky notes on the pages I want to come back to; and I attend conferences to network and meet new people face-to-face. Just as each child learns differently, so do teachers, so each teacher develops her own PLN.

Factors Preventing an Integrated Curriculum Approach

When teachers use their PLNs to seek new teaching strategies, they acquire new and innovative ways of teaching to support learning that is unique to their contexts. As they discover ideas, teachers can get particularly energized when they learn how to better integrate their units across the curriculum. Even though most teachers recognize the importance of integrating units, a number of factors can distract them from doing so, including these:

- decreased energy and motivation after professional development

- job-related stress

- focused content explored in a given area

Decreased Energy and Motivation after Professional Development

One of the books I have used most, both in my classroom and when working with other teachers, is *The Power of Guidance: Teaching Social-Emotional Skills in Early Childhood Classrooms* by Dan Gartrell (2004). This book is chock-full of concepts and strategies that help early childhood educators reflect on their approaches to behavior management in the classroom. My personal copy, though I have four more to lend others, is marked up in pen with questions, ideas, and inspirations. Sticky notes on many pages mark the importance of the content. After reading this book twice, I jotted many of my ideas and inspirations in a journal to implement at a later time. One of those ideas was to create a "peace island." A peace island is a space in the classroom that is intended to support children in exploring, developing, and experimenting with strategies to solve social conflicts. I developed a plan to get the peace island going. As the year began, I put in the effort I thought was necessary to get the routine in place. I soon discovered, though, that the children were not taking to the new routine. I assumed that I had done something wrong and gave up on the practice. It seemed as if my energy and inspiration had fizzled out.

Early childhood educators are known for assembling some of the most enthusiastic conferences. The National Association for the Education of Young Children (NAEYC) hosts an annual conference drawing approximately ten thousand attendees. The conference energy consumes several hotels surrounding a metropolitan convention center. The streets surrounding the convention become flooded with early childhood educators carrying tote bags filled with posters, books, and exciting giveaway items. Teachers, administrators, librarians, social workers, and more gather to discuss the newest and most developmentally appropriate trends, theories, and strategies for supporting children and families. When teachers attend powerful conference workshops, they become energized by the possibilities. They fervently jot down notes in their notebook or iPad app. They turn to the person next to them to talk out an idea they would like to try. Even as a presenter, I love chatting with attendees to see what I can learn from them. These notes, however, can often be forgotten once teachers get back to their settings and are reintroduced to the demands of daily operations.

Over the course of a year and after seeing Dan Gartrell present at a NAEYC conference, I found myself thinking about the peace island I had tried to implement and decided to give it another try. I revised the plan I had made for myself the year before, and I thought more intentionally about how I would introduce the tools and resources the children would have access to in the space. With consistency, confidence, and reflection, I was able to help the group adopt it as a classroom community practice for social problem solving. The experience of reading his text combined with seeing him present renewed my energy and gave me the motivation I needed to rethink and redistribute my efforts in getting this practice off and running.

Embracing professional development opportunities is important for early childhood educators. While you are participating, it's helpful to have some specific goals in mind. For example, when attending a conference, you may want to make refining your skills in teaching math a goal. You can then identify a particular area within mathematics, such as sorting by attributes, and develop a plan for how to address that goal.

Consider using the Professional Development Goal Sheet (1.1) to help focus the professional development experience. This sheet provides a space to identify the goal, determine questions, and devise a plan for exploring answers. Attending professional development events with a specific goal in mind will obviously have an impact on your choice of activities, sessions, questions, and planning. This intentional action makes the implementation of new strategies and a change in practice far more likely.

Stresses of the Job

The demands on teachers continue to increase. The reports, assessments, and surveys grow while time with children seems to dwindle. Though teachers are acquiring a louder voice advocating for more time with children and less time in front of a computer screen entering data, there still has not been much movement back toward the time teachers used to have. Planning thoughtfully and intentionally can be difficult when teachers are stressed and unfocused. When teachers think and plan in such a mind-set, it is easy to slip into an unintegrated curriculum approach, where activities and experiences are planned in silos.

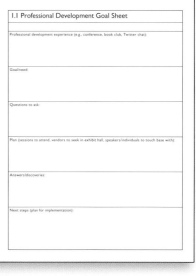

Teachers must not allow the auxiliary stresses of the job to distract them from doing what they know is best—planning and carrying out an integrated curriculum approach. If teachers can identify strategies to keep their focus on developmentally appropriate practice, they can plan more thoughtfully and reflectively. These strategies can be helpful in processing work-related stresses that can affect a teacher's focus in the classroom:

> **KEEP A JOURNAL** Jot down frustrations or questions you have around daily operations or mandates. This journal can be helpful to refer back to in times when meeting with administrators and directors.

> **FIND A COWORKER BUDDY** Finding someone at the workplace whom you can trust can be helpful. Having someone to share your thoughts with can be useful for finding solutions. This person may have a perspective on the setting or field that may be worth hearing to better understand one's own frustrations.

I keep a work journal that houses all sorts of information: questions I have for my colleagues, questions I have for myself, notes from a meeting with a group of teachers, sketches for designing classroom spaces. I started this during my first teaching job and found it extremely helpful in organizing my work life.

FIND A NON-WORK-RELATED BUDDY This individual can be just as helpful as a coworker. As this person listens to questions and frustrations, his removed point of view may be helpful in understanding a greater perspective you may have overlooked.

Remember that each of these strategies is not for everyone. Identify one that you think may work for you and give it a try. If it turns out that the first strategy did not relieve of any of your stress, try something else—eventually something will work.

Focused Content Explored in a Particular Content Area

As teachers gain new information in a particular area, they can find themselves dedicated to refining their practices in that subject area. When I was teaching preschool, I actively participated in the Early Mathematics Project as part of the Early Math Collaborative at the Erikson Institute. I discovered new ways to consider early mathematics as I planned learning experiences for my students. This intensive and long-term professional development program comprised a variety of components, such as a series of workshops deeply exploring strands of mathematics, opportunities for one-on-one support, time to collaborate with other teachers, and time to explore new manipulatives. Because of the rich content and significant time commitment involved, I found myself excited and enthusiastic about the possibilities. I found myself considering every instructional decision to be made through the lens of the math program. In doing so, I unintentionally began neglecting other areas of the curriculum. I realized that the time I spent thoughtfully planning the other subject areas began shrinking as I spent an increased amount of time planning mathematics. Having recognized this, I redistributed my planning time and restructured my thought process around the decisions I made about developing learning experiences.

While focused work on particular areas of curriculum can be powerful in teacher transformation, it can also lead teachers to focus too much on a particular area and unintentionally lift focus on another area. A common result can be less thoughtful and intentional planning in these other areas. When teachers are working diligently to improve or enhance a particular area of their teaching, they must be careful to leave nothing out in the other areas.

This book is structured in such a way that each chapter focuses on a particular subject area. Remember, each of these key elements to developing an integrated curriculum approach as you read this book.

Integrated Curriculum with a Threaded Unit Approach

Traditional approaches to curriculum in early childhood classrooms make it seem as if thematic units are planned in compartments. Units of study should be planned, however, in a way that has children learning skills in one area and then applying them in another. For example, if a kindergarten classroom is learning the attributes of basic shapes in mathematics, in art they could use pieces of tile in the basic shapes to create a mosaic. That helps to make their experiences relevant and meaningful to the skills and concepts being explored.

When I was in undergraduate school at the University of Wisconsin–La Crosse, two professors made up the majority of the early childhood program: Barb Gander and Barb Chaney. We called them "the Barbs." In their courses, they both spoke about the importance of "threading" units. They helped us understand that this was an intentional way to plan units across the year. When planned right, the units would naturally flow right into each other because the skills and concepts explored in one unit would carry over into the next. For example, if a classroom is wrapping up a unit on soils in science, the next unit may be on worms, and in reading they may have new word-wall words related to soil and worms and may explore the popular children's book *Diary of a Worm* by Doreen Cronin. The progression of content through the curriculum is natural, intentional, and contextualized. For help in the planning of a threaded unit approach, consider using the Threaded Curriculum Overview Sheet (1.2). This will help you get a view

1.2 Threaded Curriculum Overview Sheet

of the curriculum across the subject areas and determine where progression seems natural and where progression may seem disjointed.

Conclusion

My friend and colleague Peter Pizzolongo, early childhood specialist and former associate executive director for professional development for NAEYC, knows full well that play, exploration, and inquiry are at the heart of a high-quality early childhood program, and that technology should play a role in those pillars. He offers a bit of his experience and perspective:

> "Technology and interactive media are here to stay." That's a line from the position statement on technology developed by NAEYC and the Fred Rogers Center. And, as with most tools used by teachers, there are appropriate uses and inappropriate uses of technology. I've seen examples of the inappropriate uses; we all have. And we've also seen appropriate uses. An issue of *Young Children* included an article, "Classroom Bird Feeding: Giving Flight to the Imaginations of 4- and 5-Year-Olds!" In this article, the author described a play-based, exploratory, collaborative experience in which children's interest in birds led to many discoveries. Noticing many different kinds of birds attracted to a birdfeeder, the children and teacher consulted birding websites to help identify the birds. Obtaining information via the Internet is a natural occurrence for most adults—and increasingly for young children as well.
>
> I began my journey in the world of technology and young children thirty years ago. I was interested in strategies preschoolers used to understand patterns. My favorite tool for this was a set of wooden attribute blocks. The blocks differed by shape (circle, square, triangle), colors, and size (small, bigger, biggest). I would create a tic-tac-toe pattern with the blocks, such as "rows of same-size triangle, circle, square; columns of red, blue, yellow." I would remove one of the blocks and ask, "What's missing?" Noticing the two attributes, children would determine that they needed a yellow circle, or a red square, etc. As children mastered the single-object-per-cell two-attribute

pattern, I created more complex patterns for the children to analyze. That was a fairly simple activity for an educator-programmer to create on an Apple IIe. I taped colored shapes to various keys, and when a child selected the appropriate shape to fill in "what's missing," a clown would appear, waving to the successful player. The preschoolers would use the same problem-solving skills for the 3D activity and its two-dimensional complement.

Technology has come a long way since the days of the earliest classroom-sized computers, as has our understanding of how children learn. Children can continue to use various interactive programs to re-create hands-on concrete experiences via a different medium. Technology also allows children to "go places" they physically couldn't. Recently I observed children using a program to identify the spatial relationships of objects on a screen, as their point of view (POV) changed. With an "I'm standing in the corner of a room POV," a child could identify which object he deduced was closest to him. Then, the two-dimensional child floated to the ceiling. The spatial relationships among objects changed as the POV changed, and the object that initially appeared closest actually was not. Cool!

As indicated in the introduction, this book is intended to provide teachers with strategies to enhance a particular subject area with digital media and technology. While you are reading, I hope you are able to gather new tools and tips for your teaching toolbox. Moreover, I hope you are inspired to develop your own ideas and strategies and then share them in your PLN.

1 Forms

1.1 Professional Development Goal Sheet

www.redleafpress.org/techpk/1-1.pdf

1.2 Threaded Curriculum Overview Sheet

www.redleafpress.org/techpk/1-2.pdf

1.1 Professional Development Goal Sheet

Professional development experience (e.g., conference, book club, Twitter chat):

Goal/need:

Questions to ask:

Plan (sessions to attend, vendors to seek in exhibit hall, speakers/individuals to touch base with):

Answers/discoveries:

Next steps (plan for implementation):

1.2 Threaded Curriculum Overview Sheet

	Sept.	Oct.	Nov.	Dec.	Jan.	Feb.	Mar.	Apr.	May	June
Science:										
Math:										
Literacy:										
Art:										
Music:										
Social Studies:										
Health:										
Physical Education:										

From *Teaching in the Digital Age for Preschool and Kindergarten: Enhancing Curriculum with Technology* by Brian Puerling, © 2018. Published by Redleaf Press, www.redleafpress.org. This page may be reproduced for classroom use only.

Science | ②

I VIVIDLY REMEMBER A SCIENCE UNIT from when I was in elementary school, back in the late 1980s and early 1990s. The unit focused on the exploration and investigation of the rain forest. We read books and watched videos about the rain forest. We also converted the entire grade-level hallway into a rain forest. We took large cardboard tubes and turned them into tree trunks. In art class, we used papier-mâché to create animals and birds. We suspended items from the ceiling to simulate a thick canopy. Toward the end of the investigation, we took a field trip to a university in Milwaukee. During this field trip, we gathered in an auditorium with other students learning about the rain forest and had an opportunity to participate in a video conference conversation with Robert Ballard, renowned oceanographer and maritime archaeologist, while he was on location at one of his research sites in a rain forest in Belize. During the conversation, students were able to ask him questions they had come up with in their investigations. I had never seen anything like it—I could not believe that it was possible to see and talk with someone who was not standing in front of you. That experience was powerful. The inquiry-based learning process is guided by children's interest, questions, and curiosities (Gadzikowski 2013).

As children realize they are in charge of this process, they become comfortable and invested. It is powerful because young children learn best when they are immersed in the content they are exploring. And as I explored the rain forest, I was immersed in the content through art, literature, and technology. Project-based learning, an example of inquiry-based teaching, offers an opportunity for teachers to see children developing the foundations for skills necessary in the world (Kay and Greenhill 2013). Children develop skills to communicate ideas and theories, think critically, be creative, and collaborate with others.

Design Thinking in Kindergarten

Inquiry-based learning can take on many forms, one of the most notable being the project approach. Children embark on self-driven investigations of topics determined by the children in the group. This process includes research, interviews, constructing, and sharing. At Catherine Cook School in Chicago, we are always looking for more avenues into the inquiry process. We have been exploring the idea of design thinking. This approach is popular in the business field. It is typically used by corporate problem-solving firms such as IDEO (Innovation, Design Engineering Organization). Based all over the globe, IDEO helps companies and corporations explore solutions to priority issues or concerns. For example, if you walked into Walgreens today, you might notice that the pharmacist has a desk in the waiting area, rather than working behind the counter in the back with the medications (IDEO 2010). Walgreens noticed that one of their highest-paid employees was one of the least accessible individuals in the store. They wanted to determine how to make the pharmacist more accessible to customers. After working with IDEO, they identified the strategy of taking the pharmacist out from behind the counter and putting her out in front where the patrons are, making her immediately available for questions and inquiries. Walgreens has been experimenting with this approach to see if this is the solution to increasing accessibility to their pharmacists.

According to IDEO, the design-thinking process for educators can be applied to inquiry-based teaching in the classroom context and includes five parts (2012):

1. Discovery

- Identify the challenge/problem/task.

- Determine what to research and how to research it.

2. Interpretation

- Determine what was learned from the research.

- Determine how new learning informs how to move forward with the project.

3. Ideation

- Generate/brainstorm ideas for how to address the challenge, solve the problem, or tackle the task.

- Sketch out ideas.

4. Experimentation

- Give strategies/solutions a try.

- Get feedback, ask others if it makes sense.

- Make changes to plan if necessary.

5. Evolution

- Discuss how the strategies worked or did not work and why.

- Move forward and identify what's next.

Kindergarten teacher Rachel Hill took her class through the design-thinking process when she recognized that her students were interested in the rain forest. She asked them what they would like to do, and they quickly announced that they wanted to turn their classroom loft into a rain forest. They discussed what they already knew about the rain forest and used a combination of books, videos, photographs, and multi-touch mobile device applications to search for answers to questions they had. Rachel then took a picture of the classroom loft and created a planning sheet for each student. On this sheet were two images of the loft taken from different directions. The students were then to draw over

the top of the images to identify where and what should be placed on the loft to turn it into a rain forest.

Next, the students were to take their planning a step further and write down what materials around the room could be used to create those items. For example, if a child thought a river should be made for the bottom of the loft, the child needed to determine what classroom materials could be used to create it. After the children had drawn their sketches, made their plans, and gathered their materials, they broke into groups or pairs and got to work. This experience provided children with the opportunity to use their own interest as a guide for learning.

Supporting Learning: In this process, the students were invited to explore an interest in the rain forest. Their natural curiosity led them to utilize all sorts of resources to conduct research. They learned about the layers of the rain forest, common animals and insects, the climate, bodies of water, and types of trees. All of this learning was done through an interest in creating their own rain forest. I vividly remember walking into the room one day to find the entire class arranged into groups, actively working on various parts of the rain forest. Groups were working on the grass, the giant tree trunk, the winding river, the animals, and the vines. Every child was engaged and motivated.

Assessment and Documentation: Throughout the process of the children's researching and creating the rain forest, Rachel and her assistant took photographs and videos to document the experience. These photographs and videos can be evidence of a child's ability to persevere and work diligently on a task. They could also be evidence of a child's ability to collaborate with others and negotiate roles.

Sharing Learning with Others: The photographs and videos captured were shared with families so that they could witness the children's engagement and genuine enthusiasm during the research and construction. Sharing these moments are powerful for families to see as they provide families with a glimpse into the classroom and how the children are able to effectively work together. At Catherine Cook, we have guests, prospective families, and other classrooms visiting often. During these times, the students were able to show visitors what they had created and answer questions.

Exploring Space through Augmented Reality

Science is a subject area that can naturally lead to concepts that seem abstract, particularly for young children. Early childhood educators know children need concrete, hands-on experiences to process information in a developmentally appropriate way. Augmented reality provides individuals with an experience that simulates reality visually. A popular unit of study in the early years includes concepts related to planets, space, and the universe. Children are easily fascinated by the ability to leave the planet on a ship and explore space. When I was teaching preschool in the Chicago Public Schools, we worked together to create a space shuttle launchpad. The children used large connecting pieces, paper, string lighting, and wooden chairs to support them in creating a space shuttle in our dramatic play center. As mentioned in *Teaching in the Digital Age: Smart Tools for Age 3 to Grade 3* (Puerling 2012), we used a variety of resources to conduct research as to what would go into the space shuttle. At the time, we had photographs and videos to help us conduct our research. Since then, NASA has developed a new application, Spacecraft 3D. This application allows

individuals to choose a spacecraft or satellite, scan an image looking like gravel, and view the structure right in front of them on the screen. Some spacecraft provide the opportunity to operate the structural pieces. For example, users can rotate the Mars Curiosity 360 degrees. In the photo on the left, taken in a preschool classroom, the image had been printed out and placed at the bottom of this sand and water table, leaving it clear of beans enough to be scanned. Once the image was scanned, the Curiosity would appear.

We know that when children are genuinely interested in the content they are exploring, they will learn more about it. Using Doodlecast Pro (for iOS devices 10.0 or earlier) in this way will help teachers identify the unit concepts necessary to build a unit that is interesting to their groups.

This experience provides children with the opportunity to engage with a spacecraft observation center, allowing them to get as close as possible to the actual spacecraft. This application allows the user to take a photograph of what is seen on the screen. A teacher could take photos of what the students are seeing, then import them into an application called Doodlecast Pro, where images can be arranged in any sequence and teachers can record a student's questions and observations over the top of these images. As teachers create these videos, they can gather valuable information about the students' background knowledge and interests.

Supporting Learning: Early childhood educators know that young children need concrete, hands-on experiences to explore skills and concepts. Learning about planets, the solar system, and spacecraft can easily become abstract. Spacecraft 3D provides an avenue for young children to get as close as they can to these structures. As they are able to zoom in and operate some functions of the spacecraft, they are able to learn about what they can and cannot do. They can also get an idea of what the spacecraft might be made of and how it moves.

By placing the scannable marker in a sand and water table, as illustrated in the image, the children are able to have their very own spacecraft observation center.

Assessment and Documentation: Having students create background knowledge or inquiry videos using the Doodlecast Pro application, teachers can gather valuable information in regard to the students' background knowledge and interests. As teachers watch these videos, they can jot down notes concerning the students' questions and possible misconceptions. Consider using the Background Knowledge/Inquiry Video Sheet (2.1) to help you gather and organize the information you learn from these videos.

Sharing Learning with Others: As one can see, this application has the ability to take a photo of the spacecraft being viewed in the application. These photos can be taken with the children in the photo as well. These photos can be printed out and sent home, e-mailed home, put in a newsletter, or pinned on a bulletin board. Such photos sent home can be a powerful piece to generate conversation about what is happening at school.

Exploring Water In and Out of the Water Table

Young children explore cause and effect naturally in all sorts of contexts and experiences. Toddlers enjoy sitting in a high chair and watching the food drop from their hands onto the floor. At the park, children toss sand down the slide to see how it makes it to the bottom. At Catherine Cook, we observe children seeing what happens if they throw a ball over the fence of our rooftop playground. Providing children with opportunities to explore cause and effect is essential. At any age, much of what we learn in science is through experimentation. In preschool a popular science-related space in the classroom includes a water table. There children are able to fill cups with water and dump it on

other structures with traps and wheels to see what will happen. In the application Watee, children can use what they have learned at the water table to try virtually to get water into a jug. Rotating and spinning objects act as obstacles, making it a challenge to determine how and when to release the water so the user can manipulate the moving objects to his advantage to direct the water into the jug. In this experience, children are able to explore early concepts of physics and the properties of objects and water.

Supporting Learning: Water provides an experience for children to strategize and problem solve quickly. They are able to try dumping the water down through the obstacles to see what will happen. Without any cleanup, they are immediately able to try another strategy to get the water into the jug. This app provides an experience where children are able to quickly use what they learned in their trial and error and apply it to their next strategy.

Assessment and Documentation: As teachers observe children using this application, they can determine whether children are learning from the strategies they attempt. As teachers observe children working together to problem solve collaboratively, they can determine how children listen to each other's ideas and integrate them into the next strategy attempted.

Sharing Learning with Others: Children can share with other children in the class what they have learned in this application by creating a small bulletin board at eye level where they can leave tips for particular strategies. Young children have a wide range of abilities when it comes to early writing development, so these tips can be illustrated with drawings or written as young children do with letter strings. Teachers can affix a small dictation of what the children are trying to say so that when children visit the board at a later time the tips are not forgotten.

Virtual Travels

At Catherine Cook School, our kindergartners learn about Africa. In this unit of study, they explore the landscape, animals, instruments, and food of that continent. To help children explore these elements, teachers Barb Fisher and Lauren Goldberg invite guests into the classroom to discuss their experiences and knowledge of Africa and the African culture. They use Google Earth, a simple online resource, to help the children get a better idea of what the landscapes of Africa look like. Both teachers structure the experience as if the entire class were about to board a plane to fly to Africa. The chairs are arranged in rows, the children have passports stamped, and carry-on bags are stowed underneath their seats. Once on their plane, they discuss the importance of safety onboard and then take off to Africa. They have the origin location in Google Earth set to the address of our school so they can see the great distance it is to Africa.

Scan here to visit Google Earth:

Or go to www.google.com/earth.

Supporting Learning: In this experience, the children are able to access the idea of distance in a less abstract fashion. They are able to get an idea of what the African landscape looks like. They are able to see the similarities and differences between the architecture of the buildings. Young children are busy at developing their concepts of families and communities, and experiences like these help guide them in this process to arrive at a concept that is accurate and respectful. As the children move through the unit, they can refer back to this experience to help them make connections and understand new concepts when guest speakers talk about their experiences in Africa, or when they read a book or watch a video about Africa. As the children explore their dramatic play center, which is an African safari, they will have a better concept of what it would be like to actually be on a safari. This knowledge then helps them determine how they create the narrative they act out.

Assessment and Documentation: While "visiting" Africa, the children will be seeing many new things. Knowing this, teachers can end up speaking the whole time while attempting to explain everything to them. Maintaining a balance of dialogue is important. This is a good time to ask questions to learn what the students are thinking and observing. Here are some possible questions:

- What do you see here?

- What do you notice?

- What looks interesting to you here?

- What do you want to learn more about?

- Does anything confuse* you here?

- What questions do you have?

(*The word *confuse* can be difficult to understand. Be sure to have introduced this word prior to asking this question.)

Consider using the Virtual Tour Assessment Sheet (2.2) to help you organize what you learn from your students about their questions and observations.

Sharing Learning with Others: Sharing this experience with others can be done in a variety of ways. Taking photographs and video is an easy way to share this experience with families. For families with Internet access, teachers may consider providing directions to use Google Earth to visit Africa with their children at home. For those families who do not have access at home, having a computer or multi-touch mobile device available during a pickup or drop-off time would allow families to see what their children saw.

2.2 Virtual Tour Assessment Sheet			
Destination of virtual tour:			
Date:			
Stage of unit:	Beginning:	Middle:	End:
What do you see here? What do you notice?			
What looks interesting to you here?			
What do you want to learn more about?			
Does anything confuse you here?			
What questions do you have?			

Learning about Seasons through Video Conferencing

Seasons are a common area of study in early childhood classrooms. While Barb Fisher's class was learning about fall, there were many questions about what fall was like in other parts of the country. Barb's former colleague Amanda Beights was teaching preschool in Naples, Florida, and arranged a Skype conversation between the two classes. During the conversation, the children in Chicago were able to ask the preschoolers in Naples about what it was like in Florida during the fall season. Here are some of their questions:

- Does it get warmer or cooler during fall?

- Do any leaves change colors in Florida?

- Do any leaves fall to the ground?

The researchers in Chicago were surprised to learn from the children in Naples that leaves do turn colors during the fall.

Video conferencing is powerful for a couple reasons:

Consider using a document camera to compare and contrast different leaves during each season. Observe and discuss the colors, textures, and sizes. Most document cameras have a zoom in/out capability to allow students to take a close look at these characteristics.

Student Ownership

The children used the technology as a tool to support them in researching answers to questions they developed. The questions were not developed by the teacher. When children feel a sense of agency in the process of their learning, they are then naturally instilled with a genuine interest and motivation.

Students as Experts

When planning for units and investigations, teachers often overlook the idea of students being experts in their own life experiences. In this experience, the pre-schoolers in Naples were able to be the experts on their experience of seasons in their own community. They were able to answer questions and help others understand an experience with which they were not familiar.

Building Relationships

Video conferencing experiences naturally help individuals build relationships that can be utilized later for future learning. Children enjoy being around and speaking with other children, so experiences like these will make for enjoyable and meaningful conversations for sharing and learning in the future.

In science, video conferences can add a new dimension to the learning process. Consider these possibilities for places that might have individuals with whom to have video conference conversations if they are not able to visit the classroom:

- nature preserve

- aquarium

- zoo

- museum

- factory

- restaurant

- theater

- doctor's office

- veterinary clinic

Early childhood educators know that dramatic play experiences are imperative to young children's ability to process and understand perspectives, roles, responsibilities, stories, and feelings. When children are given the opportunity to create their own stories during play, they often enjoy including animals. The application Dr. PetPlay can be added to help children explore the roles and responsibilities of caring for animals. In this application, children can look at x-rays of skeletons and create profiles for the animals for which they are caring. In a veterinary clinic setup, the application provides some cues for children to discuss how the animal is feeling, its age, and if the animal is eating and drinking. This tool added to dramatic play can be what some children need to access this information and realize its importance when caring for animals. The content and structure of this app also helps elevate the level of play between the children, as they will be asking high-level questions and using appropriate vocabulary for the context.

For those very young children who are non-readers, it is important to discuss the features of the application, as they will rely on visual cues and icons to indicate the function or feature.

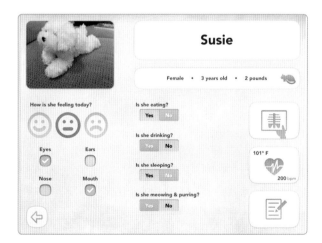

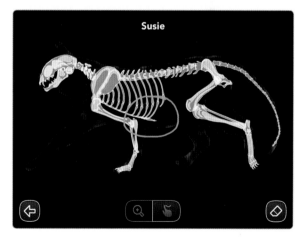

Supporting Learning: Young children are working hard to process, interpret, and understand the world around them. Dramatic play offers them a safe place to do that. They can experiment with creating different narratives to act out independently and with others. As they try on roles of new and familiar community members, they gain a better sense of the world around them. Many children have pets, and pets need to go to the veterinarian, just as children need to go to the doctor. Having this experience will help the children better understand the roles and intentions of veterinarians. This understanding can be helpful when taking pets to a veterinarian or when visiting the doctor for their own needs.

Assessment and Documentation: As teachers observe the children, they can listen for the children's use of new vocabulary, their ability to create and act out a narrative that makes sense for the roles they have chosen, and their ability to work with others to negotiate these roles and be flexible in changing the narrative as the play continues. These elements are important for social-emotional development and early writing development.

Sharing Learning with Others: The dramatic play experience of playing doctor is very popular with young children. This play often ends up with children caring for animals as doctors would care for children. It might be helpful to share this application with families so they can engage in conversation about future visits to the doctor or the veterinarian. If the child has experience with the application, the parents will get an idea if the child is able to use new vocabulary and understand the roles and responsibilities for caring for others, animals and humans.

Green Screening and Stop-Motion Videos

In Michael Lin's developmental kindergarten class at The Willows Community School in Culver City, California, the students learn about penguins. They learn about their habitat, life cycle, and food. Michael plans all sorts of experiences for the children to understand the lives of penguins. As mentioned earlier, dramatic play is a crucial part of an early childhood program. Therefore, one of those experiences Michael plans is to invite the children to dress up as penguins and record a video with a green screen in the background, with a superimposed image of what would be the habitat of the penguins they are learning about. They are also able to make sock puppets to create a story with the same green screen background. A green screen effect can be achieved by using a camera and a photo program such as Photo Booth on Apple products and in Windows Movie Maker for PCs.

Michael also provides the students with the opportunity to sculpt clay models of penguins and then record stop-motion videos with an application such as iMotion HD, Stop Motion Studio, or iStopMotion. In these videos, they are able to share what they have learned about penguins and create stories that would be common in the life of a penguin.

Supporting Learning: In these experiences, the children are able to utilize what they are learning to create realistic stories about penguins. To create a realistic narrative around a penguin, the student would have to have a firm understanding of the animal's habitat, life cycle, and food.

Assessment and Documentation: As Michael reviews these videos, he is able to get an idea of what the children are learning about penguins. The content of the narratives the children create provide him with valuable information about how the children are able to pull this information together and generate and demonstrate an understanding through these videos.

Sharing Learning with Others: Michael believes that parent communication is essential, and he establishes a lot of avenues to make that happen. He creates DVDs for the families that include clips of significant classroom experiences. He also shares the full videos with families so they can learn about penguins from their children. These videos are also good tools for generating discussion about what is going on at school.

Conclusion

As mentioned earlier, young children need concrete, hands-on experiences to develop skills and explore concepts. Science is a very interesting area for many young children, but the somewhat abstract nature of it can turn some children off or make it difficult to understand. Technology can help make some areas of science more accessible and interesting to younger learners.

Forms

2

2.1 Background Knowledge/Inquiry Video Sheet

www.redleafpress.org/techpk/2-1.pdf

2.2 Virtual Tour Assessment Sheet

www.redleafpress.org/techpk/2-2.pdf

2.1 Background Knowledge/Inquiry Video Sheet

Child's name:	Date:

Video type: Background knowledge / Inquiry

Questions:

Possible misconceptions:

Other notes for planning future learning experiences:

Child's name:	Date:

Video type: Background knowledge / Inquiry

Questions:

Possible misconceptions:

Other notes for planning future learning experiences:

2.2 Virtual Tour Assessment Sheet

Destination of virtual tour:

Date:

Stage of unit:	Beginning:	Middle:	End:

What do you see here? What do you notice?

What looks interesting to you here?

What do you want to learn more about?

Does anything confuse you here?

What questions do you have?

Mathematics | 3

I REMEMBER WHEN I WAS VERY YOUNG, sitting on the couch with my grand-mother. We had just finished playing a board game. She was babysitting me while my mom was away. I had asked her how long it was going to be before my mother would be home. She looked at the clock and said it would be two hours. I had just started learning how to tell time in school, so I was developing the early foundational concepts of time past and counting ahead. It was about noon at the time of our conversation, and according to my grandmother, my mom was due back at around two p.m. I proceeded to say she was incorrect—it would be, in fact, three hours until she was to be back. I counted on the clock, beginning with 12:00: "One (pointing to 12:00), two (pointing to 1:00), three (pointing to 2:00)." She then recounted for me, showing me that when count-ing, you only reach one when the long hand has made a complete

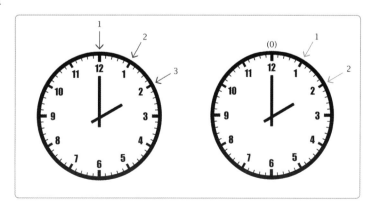

circle around the clock. She demonstrated, starting at 12:00, saying, "one" and ending at 1:00. Then, "two" while making the circle from 1:00 to 2:00. I was a bit surprised to learn that I had misunderstood this concept, but it made sense when she showed me in this way. Young children need concrete and hands-on experiences to best explore new concepts, particularly when they are abstract.

Early childhood educators are constantly looking for high-quality ways to support young children in their acquisition of early mathematics concepts. Recent publications such as Amy Shillady's *Spotlight on Young Children: Exploring Math* (2012) and programs such as the Early Math Collaborative, mentioned earlier, have been putting forth substantial efforts to help the field provide children with the necessary experiences to develop solid foundations in mathematics.

As we think and plan, considering how technology can enhance these experiences is important. Teachers and children can use a variety of tools and resources to explore concepts, capture learning as it happens, and share it with others. Technology undoubtedly can provide children with new experiences that can make mathematics interesting and understandable.

Capturing Learning through Video

The camera app on any multi-touch mobile device can be a tool to help students record their thinking and processing. When helping young children explore early mathematic concepts, early childhood educators ask questions and provide experiences where the children can describe their thinking and understanding. For example, sorting objects into groups is a common skill learned in the early years. A teacher may record a video of the child sorting counting bears by size or color while having the child say why he is choosing each bear for each group. This video and others taken will be valuable samples to review when planning for future experiences regarding sorting and attributes. These videos can also be used later during parent-teacher conferences.

After recording, watch the video with the child. As the child watches himself share what he was thinking, the child may self-correct or add another detail that he did not mention or point out during the recording. This experience helps the child value and understand the foundations of self-assessment and self-reflection.

When recording, I have found that using a device mount of some kind is helpful because it provides a hands-free experience to be able to fully engage with the child. The child can also see herself so she is aware of what is happening with the device.

Supporting Learning: These videos help young children begin to explore the idea of self-assessment. Children begin to learn that when listening to what they had previously said, they may have said something incorrectly or inaccurately and want to rerecord so that it is articulated correctly. In doing so, they are learning the value of paying attention to details when explaining things to others.

Assessment and Documentation: As a teacher watches these videos, she can listen to the child's thinking and determine whether the child is accurately understanding the concept being explored and taught. If a teacher determines that the child does not fully understand the concept, she can develop individualized activities or experiences for that child.

Sharing Learning with Others: These videos can be shared in many ways: via e-mail, DVD, flash drive, or QR code, or uploaded to YouTube or Vimeo and shared with URL links. At Catherine Cook, we use Vimeo to share videos that are larger in file size or that we want to share with a larger audience. We particularly like Vimeo because it provides users with the ability to add a password to access the videos. As are the teachers, families seeing these videos are given an opportunity to listen in on the child's thinking and articulation of their ideas.

Spatial Sense and Construction with Stop-Motion Videos

Boys and girls enjoy visiting the block center to integrate building materials and figurines to create a narrative. As the children find new pieces, their narrative may change directions. As they build their structures, other children enter the area and say, "Wow, how did you build that?" When parents come to pick up their children, they often ask the same question. We can help answer this question and share the story of how structures were built by creating stop-motion videos. iMotion HD and I Can Animate are applications that make creating these videos easy. Set up the multi-touch mobile device in a way that will capture the space where the building is occurring—a mount is recommended but not required. The children take a photograph every so often. The app then compiles the photographs and plays them back at fast speed, creating a video.

As mentioned above, these videos can be kept and uploaded to a web storage resource such as YouTube or Vimeo. Once they are uploaded, a teacher can take the links for these videos and create a QR code for each video, using QR code scanning and a generation application such as QR Reader by Tapmedia. These QR codes can be placed next to pictures of the finished structures on pages in a binder, which can be housed in the block center. When children are looking for some ideas of what to build, they can use the binder for ideas by scanning the QR codes and watching the videos. Another option is to take a video of the children verbally describing how they created the structure. These videos too can be uploaded and linked to QR codes, which can be accessed in the binder.

Supporting Learning: As children make and watch videos, they learn that towers can take a lot of time to build. Having this awareness can help children build empathy for others who put effort into something they created. It can also help them learn to appreciate other children's strengths and abilities. The construction of these towers requires knowledge regarding what makes a good, sturdy tower, as well as a degree of spatial sense. As children review these videos with other children or adults, they can articulate their process and decision making.

To help children avoid forgetting to take a photo every so often, consider giving them a timer to set for one minute. When the timer goes off, they are reminded that it is time to take another photograph.

These images and QR codes can also be placed on a bulletin board in the hallway so that parents and visitors can take a closer look at what is happening in the classroom.

Assessment and Documentation: These videos can provide teachers with information about how children are able to articulate their process of creating their structures. This information could be referring to the vocabulary used or the sequence they described. Watching these videos over the course of the year will also help teachers determine if the structures are becoming more sophisticated and detailed. If teachers determine that the structures are not progressing in detail and complexity, they can plan some activities or experiences that may help nudge the children to do more. Possible experiences include watching a video of a construction site or inviting an older child to join in on the building process. Consider using the Block Structure Complexity Sheet (3.1) to help keep track of this progression.

Sharing Learning with Others: Linking these videos to QR codes is a quick way to share the videos with a large audience, whether in the classroom, in the hallway, or in a newsletter. If these videos are uploaded to YouTube or Vimeo, the links can easily be e-mailed as well. Not all families have access to smartphone technology or the Internet, so be prepared to share them in other ways, such as with a DVD or by looping on a computer monitor at a pickup and drop-off location.

Sharing Process and Thinking through Video Whiteboard

Considering how content and experiences can be integrated throughout the subject areas is important. In chapter 2, I mentioned Doodlecast Pro, an application that allows individuals to bring audio, images, and illustrations together to create a video. Preschool and kindergarten teachers can use this application to invite children to share what and how they have created something. For example, with our four-year-olds, we do such recordings several times over the course of the year as a digital work sample to help families observe growth in articulation, use of vocabulary, and demonstration of skills.

Scan this QR code to view a great demonstration of how to use Doodlecast Pro (for iOS devices 10.0 or earlier):

 Or go to www.youtube.com/watch?v=ZsD5aCTvfGY.

Supporting Learning: In this experience, the children are learning how to recall details and describe them so that others can understand the sequence. They are also learning how to tell a story that makes sense, or in a way that follows natural cause and effect. In terms of math, they needed to use certain geometric vocabulary to describe how they used their shapes creatively to illustrate a garden.

Assessment and Documentation: Upon reviewing these videos, teachers would be able to identify whether the children are using new vocabulary correctly. They would learn about the children's ability to be descriptive about what choices they made and the processes they followed, and their ability to recall the sequence of events effectively.

Sharing Learning with Others: The teacher of the class where the shape gardens were made used these videos as a work sample during parent-teacher conferences. Videos with children articulating process and telling stories provide very rich material for conversation in terms of progress, development, goals, and opportunities for teacher-parent partnerships. A video provides an experience where the teacher and parents can have a shared understanding of where the particular child is at and how to move forward together.

Creating Number Stories

Young children often learn new concepts in the context of a story. When I taught pre-school, I introduced the mathematical concept of matching sets with the book *Seaweed Soup* (2001) by Stuart Murphy. This book became extremely popular and one we liked to read before lunch each day. To help themselves identify their own ways to apply new concepts to daily life, children can create their own number stories. Amanda Burns invited her kindergarten students to create number stories using the Book Creator application. This user-friendly application makes it easy for children to import images, draw pictures, and add audio and video to their stories. In these experiences, these young mathematicians can create their own e-books of number stories they have created. If students were to start on their stories in the beginning of the year and continue to add to them over the course of the year, they could be used as evidence of growth over time. (More examples for how Book Creator can be used will be discussed in chapter 4, which explores literacy.)

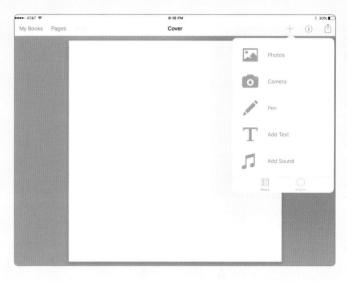

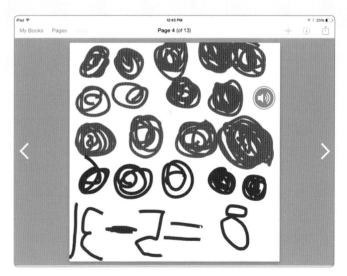

Supporting Learning: As the children develop and illustrate their number stories, we encourage them to repeat the stories out loud. This is important because hearing your thought process as an inner monologue is different than hearing it aloud. We have found that as the children speak their stories aloud, they are more likely to catch errors they made.

3.2 Number Story e-Book Complexity Sheet				
Child:	Date:	Last number sentence:	Most recent number sentence:	Page number:

Assessment and Documentation: As the children add to number stories, they develop their own number story e-book. Book Creator is structured in a way that as you pass through the book, moving from page to page, you see the number stories over time. From an assessment standpoint, this is an authentic sample that includes illustrations and audio of the children articulating their stories, number sentences, and solutions. As teachers review these, they can determine if students are repeating certain mistakes and progressing in the complexity of their number stories. Consider using the Number Story e-Book Complexity Sheet (3.2) to help you organize your notes on the progression of complexity of number stories for your students.

Sharing Learning with Others: Book Creator allows you and your students to share the e-books in a few ways. You can export them to the multi-touch mobile device's bookshelf, e-mail the books to anyone who has iBooks, export them as PDFs, and e-mail them. You can also download Calibre, an e-book management system that anyone using iOS, Windows, or Linux can use to view these books. When families have access to these books, they too can see the progress being made in their children's mathematical skill development. Please note that Calibre will only allow you to view e-books in a way that does not include video or audio features.

Exporting the e-book as a PDF will not include any audio features the student included.

Scan here to download Calibre:

Or go to http://calibre-ebook.com/download.

Demystifying Electronics

In this digital age, children are engaging with technology every day in some capacity. But usually there is not a lot of conversation that helps children understand how these technologies work. The computer is the magic black box;

the iPad is the magic tablet. In my work with children at Catherine Cook, I hope to help our young learners understand how these machines work. Simply searching for and showing children photographs of computers, laptops, and tablets once the cases and glass have been removed can be quite insightful. When showing these to young children, I speak in the most general terms. Much of the conversation is related to messages being sent back and forth. For example, "When you touch the iPad in a certain place, it sends the iPad a message telling it what do to." These conversations can be quite insightful for teachers as well. I remember facilitating this conversation with a kindergarten class and being astounded at what they already knew regarding how machines work. I learned that not being afraid to ask them questions about these evolving technologies is important.

Supporting Learning: Young children often think that computers, tablets, laptops, smartphones, or GPS devices are almost magical. They have solid ideas about what they can do but not about how those devices actually do those things. In this experience, I helped the children explore some of the truth behind how some of these electronics work. In chapter 2, I discussed how abstract concepts are difficult for young children to comprehend, so putting these concepts in terms they can understand, such as a message being sent, makes them more accessible and understandable.

Assessment and Documentation: In this experience, I assessed based on the actual conversations I had with children, using the recordings as documentation. I asked a lot of questions so that the children could offer me and their peers their thinking about how mobile technologies and related tablet electronics work. I was quite surprised at how much they knew! This conversation was very helpful as we planned the next activities for their math stations.

Sharing Learning with Others: After uploading our video to YouTube or Vimeo, I could share with other early childhood teachers in the school during a faculty meeting to help them get an idea of what our kindergartners are thinking in terms of electronics. First-grade teachers would benefit from seeing this as well so they can get an idea of the background knowledge, experiences, and ideas that the kindergartners already have. If shared with families, they too would see the foundation of knowledge their children have. In addition, families could better contextualize and understand the future activities and experiences we would engage in during math stations.

Exploring Early Programming Logic

Ever since the popular code.org video was released that advocated for computer science across curriculum, there has been much talk about how to integrate the early foundations of programming in elementary curriculum. New tools are emerging that provide children with opportunities to explore these concepts directly; however, several standard early childhood classroom routines are already in place that are laying these foundations:

- following directions
- giving directions
- sequencing
- organizing items in a cubby or locker
- building with blocks

- sorting objects into groups

- honoring trial and error

- nurturing imagination

These classroom practices provide children with experiences that will later help them explore more explicit concepts related to early programming.

Scan this QR code to visit code.org and learn more:

Or go to https://code.org/educate.

Board Games

Young children love games of all kinds, whether impromptu games made up on the playground, I Spy games on road trips, or board games. Games provide children with the opportunity to learn new skills and concepts in a context that is exciting and meaningful. They provide tangible and concrete experiences that make accessing new content developmentally appropriate. With increased interest in integrating coding/programming skills into curriculum has come efforts to identify developmentally appropriate entry points for young children as well. Not many board games have been developed for young children; however, one notable game is Robot Turtles. This game helps children come closer to exploring the concepts of coding and programming more directly. The object of the game is to follow the directions on the playing cards to program the turtle to get to a certain place on the game board. To learn more about this game, take a look at this video.

Scan here to view a video about Robot Turtles:

Or go to https://youtu.be/RHjB9XQodzE.

Supporting Learning: Robot Turtles provides a concrete, hands-on, and tangible experience to access the concepts and ideas of coding and programming. Sequencing with directions is the largest goal of the game and provides a strong foundation for the next steps in understanding the basics of coding and programming.

Assessment and Documentation: This game would be most successful with the involvement of and interaction with an adult or older child. This involvement would mean that a certain level of scaffolding, questioning, and encouragement would be part of the experience.

Sharing Learning with Others: Other than having children retell the story of how the game unfolded, photographs and video are the best ways to share the board game experience with others. Children are usually quite eager to tell others about how their game went, retelling who made what choice and how it impacted the rest of the game. These stories can be captured with video or even a simple memo-recording application on a smartphone. These memos can be e-mailed off to other family members who were not present for the game when it happened.

Non-textual Programming

Earlier I mentioned IDEO, an innovative firm for corporate problem solving. A few years ago, I was able to visit IDEO in Chicago. During my visit, I saw an image of a wooden programming interface for young children. I had to learn more about it. I hopped online and found the creator, Filippo Yacob. His company, Primo Toys, in London, is creating amazing tools and experiences for young children to explore early programming logic. They recently came out with Cubetto, the wooden interface I saw at IDEO. Children use wooden puzzle pieces to program a robot to move to a certain destination determined by the child.

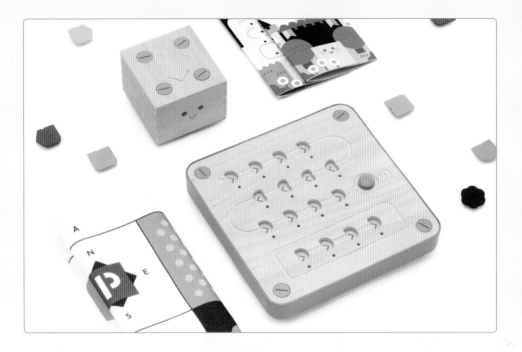

Scan here to look at this video on how a child uses Cubetto:

Or go to www.youtube.com/watch?v=xajyScKYwcw.

Filippo and I have had several chats over the years, and I now work more directly with him in his product development. He has some interesting perspectives that I think others should know:

Programming is today the beating heart of engineering, mechanics, architecture, media, and the arts. We use programming to command the machines that help us communicate instantly over a phone or a computer, design buildings that withstand earthquakes, fly airplanes, and guide us with our GPS systems when we drive in our cars. It is highly technological and scientific work, so no wonder this coveted skill among employers of a modern workforce presents a dilemma for educators. How does one go about introducing a highly scientific and deeply abstract topic to a young child between the ages of three and seven?

Learning to program can begin at an early age, by imparting logical thinking and an analytical mind-set onto a child. We look at programming in the same way we look at language, only this language is the one we use to communicate with machines, and rather than being about letters and sounds, it's about sequences. The above question becomes easier when we start thinking about programming that way. A program is a sequence of logical instructions that a machine interprets to produce an outcome, and this principle is the same, from the simplest of programs to the most complex. This also applies to life, and not just to computers and machines as explained above. For example, if you want to "program" a child to get dressed, you would ask him to put socks and underwear on before trousers and shoes. If the sequence of instructions was reversed, the outcome would be different and we would all look a little silly.

We understand three key insights which became the rules we then followed to design our experience in a way. The three insights were

1. Children learn through play.

2. Children enjoy and need challenges.

3. Children find abstract concepts difficult.

A physical play set allows children to explore logical sequencing in a tangible nonabstract way and also gives them an immediate reference to programming in the real world by programming a machine—in this case, a little robot. When thinking about programming logic, sequencing is far and beyond the most important logical aspect, but on a more direct level, sequencing becomes important in programming when children are able to understand how concepts like algorithms and programs work in practice, which they can explore for the first time using the play set.

Filippo is a developer and creator who thinks about the child's mind. He understands the way children think and play. He values that play is important and needs to be a part of this process.

The Bee-Bot, made by Terrapin Software, is another tool that helps children explore these early concepts. In a kindergarten classroom, I worked with some small groups during math, and the children created programs to send the Bee-Bot to certain places on a grid map that we created. The map was of the early childhood floor. The children were able to draw classrooms or other spaces and place them accordingly on the map. The children then choose which place to program the robot to go.

In this experience, the children were programming in a context that was relatable and contextualized. Because the Bee-Bot requires the programmer to remember the program, I provided the children with clipboards so they could write them down to remember them. These images are some of the programs they created.

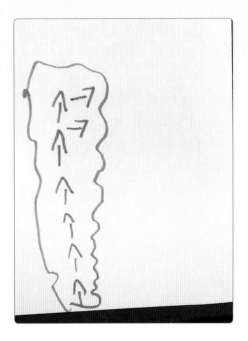

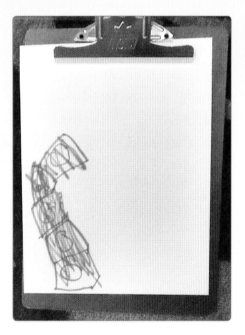

Supporting Learning: In this experience, the children were able to simultaneously develop map skills and mathematical thinking skills as they developed programs to move the Bee-Bot from one space on the map to another. As they tried out their programs and found that they did not always work, they collaborated and discussed what changes could be made to their program to make the Bee-Bot get to where they wanted it to go.

Assessment and Documentation: As I heard the group self-talk themselves through their programs, make predictions, and make changes to their programs, I took notes to help me determine where each child was at; for example, were any of them exhibiting any misconceptions, or do some need more challenging programming activities to continue to further their learning? I learned the answer was yes to both questions.

Sharing Learning with Others: As you can see in the previous photos, I had the children write down their programs. The Bee-Bot requires children to hold the program in their head, so to make sure they would not forget their programs, I had them write them down. It was interesting to see how they decided to draw them on the paper. These illustrated programs are a clear window into how they were processing these early programming concepts. I shared these with other teachers at Catherine Cook and other schools to help them see and understand how young children might process this information, challenge, and experience.

Early programming is going to continue to be a topic discussed in the field of education. We must not fear it, for there are developmentally appropriate ways to help children begin thinking about these concepts.

Conclusion

As I indicated with science, mathematics is a natural subject area in which to integrate technology. A variety of tools and resources can be utilized to help children explore and develop an understanding of mathematical relationships. The range of tools is wide sweeping, including pattern blocks, board games, measuring scales, multi-touch mobile applications, and programmable robots. The possibilities are endless.

3 Forms

3.1 Block Structure Complexity Sheet

www.redleafpress.org/techpk/3-1.pdf

3.2 Number Story e-Book Complexity Sheet

www.redleafpress.org/techpk/3-2.pdf

3.1 Block Structure Complexity Sheet

Quarter 1

Video date:	Describe observed detail and complexity:	New details and complexities since previous video (e.g., increased tower height, incorporation of bridges):

Needed experiences to nudge complexity and detail:

Quarter 2

Video date:	Describe observed detail and complexity:	New details and complexities since previous video (e.g., increased tower height, incorporation of bridges):

Needed experiences to nudge complexity and detail:

3.1 Block Structure Complexity Sheet (continued)

Quarter 3

Video date:	Describe observed detail and complexity:	New details and complexities since previous video (e.g., increased tower height, incorporation of bridges):

Needed experiences to nudge complexity and detail:

Quarter 4

Video date:	Describe observed detail and complexity:	New details and complexities since previous video (e.g., increased tower height, incorporation of bridges):

Needed experiences to nudge complexity and detail:

3.2 Number Story e-Book Complexity Sheet

Child:	Date:	Last number sentence:	Most recent number sentence:	Page number:

Literacy
(Language, Reading, and Writing)

4

WHEN I WAS IN MY THIRD YEAR at the University of Wisconsin–La Crosse, I had the assignment of creating a literacy-based experience for preschool-age children. I wanted to challenge myself and think outside the box, as much as a preservice teacher could. I began thinking about what stories are enjoyed by children and also what ones tend to scare certain children. One of the stories was *Where the Wild Things Are* by Maurice Sendak. I wondered if there was a way to retell this story that would nurture the enjoyment of those who liked the story but also provide an enjoyable experience for children tentative about it. I came up with the idea to create a shadow puppet experience, using a flashlight, muslin fabric, and cardboard character cutouts. In small groups, I retold the story with the shadow puppets, and the children seemed to enjoy it. Had I been the classroom teacher, I would have placed the materials in the classroom library so they could retell the story to each other.

In this experience, the puppets were cut out of black paper, intentionally leaving out the faces and character textures that led to the fears. Having simply black cutouts allowed the children to recognize the characters but focus their attention on the story events rather than what they feared about the characters' appearances.

Young children develop a love for reading when they are provided with rich experiences to explore children's literature. Some examples include:

- read-alouds (whole group, small group, and one-on-one)

- hand/finger puppets for retelling

- author visits to school/classroom/center

- opportunities to write their own books

- videos of books

- audiobooks

- materials for illustrating story events

- opportunities to act out stories in dramatic play center

- sand and water table activities with story character figurines

- clay or playdough to sculpt characters

Catherine Cook School is a member of the Lake Michigan Association of Independent Schools. This group convenes a few times a year to discuss pertinent topics for independent schools and education. After attending some of these meetings, I met Elisa Gall, who at the time was the Lower School librarian at the Latin School of Chicago. Upon meeting her, I learned she was married to Catherine Cook's librarian, Patrick Gall. Elisa and I have had a few conversations here and there about the appropriate uses of technology in the classroom, at home, and, of course, in the library. Libraries are a powerful space to utilize technology to support inquiry, literacy, and students' love for learning. There have been some substantial efforts to help support these initiatives by Cen Campbell of Little eLit, Renee Hobbs of the Media Education Lab at the University of Rhode Island, and Claudia Haines of the Homer Public Library in Alaska and the Association for Library Services to Children (ALSC). Elisa offers her perspective on the uses of technology and digital media in the library space:

> Some people think of libraries as simple warehouses for materials, but this couldn't be further from the truth. Students are consumers in libraries, but also thoughtful and ethical curators and creators. Amid the ever-evolving educational landscape, my school library's mission is unchanging: to stimulate and develop self-directed learning in each student and to empower community members to enact curriculum. Our focus is on information access,

use, and evaluation, as well as nurturing curiosity and a lifelong love of reading, learning, and discovery. Technology can be an effective tool to help achieve these goals and more.

In preschool story times, technology provides multiple access points to learning. Through literature apps, I've been able to connect children with books and each other. Even though many preschoolers can't yet read, read-to-me functions help children select their own stories and discover them with peers, asking questions and reading closely. Discussing the differences between oral, print, and digital formats opens doors for children to come to new understandings about how we can communicate ideas and share information.

In collaboration with teachers, I've been able to make thinking visible through digital documentation tools, including drawn responses using Doodle Buddy, oral statements on iTalk Recorder, or videos taken from an iPad camera. Technology can also empower students by providing them with information to guide reading choices. An app such as Level It Books, for example, can make finding a title's reading level as easy as scanning its ISBN. When my colleagues and I realized that learning the steps of "The Three Little Pigs" tale is not unlike the logic structure of sequence in computer programming, we started using shared vocabulary and a Bee-Bot robot to match

students' retellings of the story to the path they wanted the robot to take along our carpet. In this case, the robot was a tool that helped us to integrate science, logic, and literacy.

New media allows libraries to extend their reach beyond the walls of the school. Through remote access to our digital e-library, learners can download to and use resources on their personal devices. Students might also borrow preloaded e-readers from our circulating collection. Families can find recommendations in a myriad of convenient ways, including links from our library's Pinterest boards or video booktalks shared on our school's intranet. Services have expanded too. In a summer engagement program, my students select weekly challenges and send evidence of completion back to me. At the end of each week, I compile and publish a slideshow celebrating all of the exploration that has occurred. This type of digital outreach keeps the library open when its physical doors are closed.

The technologies I've found most successful are those that bring learners together and create unique experiences that aren't achievable otherwise. Technology can motivate students, inform them, connect them, and inspire them to learn with content areas to strengthen understandings and ask new questions. New media can do a lot of the things that print media can do, but there are surely differences. Regarding the "digital versus print" or "screen versus no screen" debates, I believe there is room for all formats to coexist and complement one another in our diverse world. No format is all-inclusive, which makes choices even more important. Variety ensures access.

Technology, both traditional and modern, has a wide range of possibilities to help support early literacy development (Casbergue and Strickland 2016). Today's tools invite children to create e-books, comics, news shows, and even their own applications. Across all grades, teachers are looking for new additional ways and entry points for children to learn, share their learning, and nurture a love for reading.

Following the Interests of Young Readers

When I was teaching, I wanted my students to begin developing mental imagery when reading stories. To do that, I began reading chapter books. We started with the Magic Tree House series by Mary Pope Osbourne. After enjoying several of those books, we moved on. When I was doing my course-work at the Erikson Institute, I learned about the Willimena Rules! series by Valerie Wilson Wesley. I introduced it to the children, and they enjoyed this series as well. After we finished the first book, I decided to ask them what they wanted to do next. As a class, we went online to find out what our next read was going to be. Today most online booksellers allow you to look at a few pages before buying. So we took a look at some of the books in this series and read a few pages. We read until we came to one that sparked our interest. Together we added it to the cart, and I used a gift card to pay for the book. Over the course of the next few days, we tracked the package. We went online to see if our package had shipped and then looked at a map to see where the truck was that carried it. When the package arrived, we enthusiastically opened it together and read the first chapter. Upon reflecting on this experi-ence, I believe it honored the children as readers with a voice and an opinion. Collaboratively, we decided how we would move forward with our shared reading experiences. The children also were able to see the process of online ordering and what that looks like.

Supporting Learning: Most children use the Internet to access games and entertainment media. In this experience, however, the children are able to see that the Internet can provide them access to materials that might not be avail-able in their immediate community. Ordering books online expands the ability to experience literature that might not be available at a nearby store or library.

Assessment and Documentation: As teachers help children understand the many uses of the Internet, they can begin to provide the students with opportunities that may invite the use of online sources to gather information. For example, perhaps a class was discussing the potential of taking a field trip to go see a play at the Emerald City Theatre in Chicago. The teacher might

4.1 Internet Features and Functions Record Sheet		
Date:	Feature/function:	Revisit in near future:
		Yes / No
		Yes / No
		Yes / No
		Yes / No
		Yes / No
		Yes / No
		Yes / No

ask the class, "How do you think we could find out plays that are now showing, their dates, and their times?" If the children were to respond with answers such as "Call them on the phone" or "Look them up the Internet," this would indicate that the children were implementing their new understandings of the purposes of the Internet into their daily lives.

Sharing Learning with Others: Consider using the Internet Features and Functions Record Sheet (4.1) to help you keep track of what you have shown your group and whether it might be necessary to revisit those features in the near future to assure understanding.

Trying Out an Author's Style

Mo Willems is a popular children's author, as young children connect so well with his characters. His application Don't Let the Pigeon Run This App! provides young readers with a few opportunities to engage with his texts. One feature includes a tutorial, led by Mo, showing how to draw a pigeon. Once the pigeon is drawn, it can be saved to the Camera Roll. Once in the Camera Roll, it can be accessed by other applications. If a child were to open the application Drawing Pad, she could draw in her own speech bubbles, as Mo uses so thoughtfully in his books. The same pigeon can be used over and over, so children can make multiple pages with the pigeon saying whatever they would like in the speech bubbles. These illustrations can then be saved to Camera Roll as well. Earlier I mentioned the Book Creator application. Writers can use Book Creator to then create their own e-books with the illustrations they made in Drawing Pad. Once they have imported the new illustrations with the speech bubbles, the writers can add audio by recording what the pigeon is saying. Another application where children can record over images is SonicPics. In both of the applications, the e-book and video can then be shared with the class and families.

Supporting Learning: For young children to see themselves as young authors and illustrators, they need to be able to make connections to the ones they enjoy and love. They need to see that authors are people who are learning as well, just learning different things. When teachers give children the opportunity to try to create similar work done by these authors, they are able to make some of these necessary connections. When children try out Eric Carle's style of collage art, they feel a sense of accomplishment. When they can draw their own pigeon with the help of Mo Willems, add their own speech bubbles, and record audio to it, they feel another sense of accomplishment.

Assessment and Documentation: As the children create these e-books, teachers can observe and confer with the children to learn more about their identity development as writers and illustrators. These one-on-one moments are also important in learning where each child is at with his early writing development as well. In these observations and conversations, teachers can learn a great deal about a child's strengths, areas of opportunity, and where she may have reluctance or fear. Consider using the Early Writer's Conference Sheet (4.2) to help you organize your notes to help with future planning and goal setting for each student.

4.2 Early Writer's Conference Sheet			
Child:	Date:	Content of conference:	Next step(s):

Sharing Learning with Others: All of these applications mentioned in this strategy have the ability to e-mail the illustrations students create. Book Creator has the ability to e-mail the EPUB book if it has audio features and also e-mail it as a PDF if there are no audio features. Sharing this work with families so that they can see this identity development unfold is important. If families are aware of the rich literacy experiences happening in the classroom, they are more likely to think about how they can create similar experiences that are just as nurturing at home.

Other applications can also be used to help young children create e-books. In the application Intro to Words, children can create pages by arranging single

letters, letter blends, and images. This application can be helpful for children who are having difficulty drawing or writing their own letters. Tablet computers and multi-touch mobile devices can offer a writing output as well as help students practice keyboarding skills (Lange 2013). The pages created can be saved into Camera Roll by taking a screenshot. These screenshots in Camera Roll can be imported into the above applications and recorded over and then shared. Felt Board is another application where children can create scenes using the collage pieces in the application. The scenes can be saved to Camera Roll and then accessed there with the other recording and publishing applications. Some children may prefer to use actual felt-board pieces and then take a snapshot of their scenes with the device.

Publishing Comics and Newsletters

ComicBook! by 3DTOPO Inc. is an application that allows children to create image collages. The images used can be photographs taken of people or of artwork made with materials. They may be illustrations created in other applications such as Drawing Pad, Intro to Words, or Don't Let the Pigeon Run This App! Users can add captions or speech bubbles to the collages, with the help of an adult or older child. In doing so, children can create their own storyboards. Teachers often use a newsletter as a way to communicate the announcements and classroom happenings. Rather than have the newsletter be completely created by the teacher, consider inviting the children to create it. For example, children could create a collage of animals seen at a zoo during a field trip. The captions could include descriptions of the animals' sounds, size, color, and texture. These newsletters can be e-mailed to families or printed out if families do not have access to e-mail or the Internet. This is an excellent way to empower the children to share the important things happening in the classroom and a way to help strengthen the classroom community as well.

Teachers may consider inviting small groups of children to create these comics or newsletters. As children work together collaboratively, they learn about each other and from each other (Castek and Kretschmar 2013). They utilize each other's strengths and interests to benefit the group.

Supporting Learning: In this experience, the young writers and reporters are able to share what is happening in their classroom in a simple but pointed way. Often teachers choose what will be shared with families in a newsletter, but in experiences like these, the children are given the opportunity to identify what they would like to share with families about what is going on in the classroom. As these newsletters are shared, the children learn more about each other. Having a stronger understanding of what is interesting to other children will help them make connections and develop friendships.

ComicBook! has a sticker feature that allows the creator to add certain stickers. I would recommend reviewing these comic-related stickers before giving this application to children to use. You may consider disabling the possibly age-inappropriate stickers.

Assessment and Documentation: As the children create their comics and newsletters, teachers can review what the children find the most interesting. This information can help in determining what experiences are most motivating and what content is most interesting. It will also be helpful in planning structures and timelines for already identified units and for identifying potential units based on the observed interests.

Sharing Learning with Others: ComicBook! offers several ways to share the comics, via e-mail, Twitter, Facebook, and Instagram. It even has a feature that enables the user to print the comics directly from application itself. Having this flexibility in sharing these creations makes it easier for families, other classrooms, and the greater community to receive the news!

Using Legos to Build Stories

This notion of building something that will not look exactly like the real thing may be helpful for children who are having difficulties coming to terms with their drawing abilities. Children often get frustrated when they are not able to draw what they have envisioned in their minds. With a combination of experiences with Legos and some conversations about the varying style of illustrators, these children can become comfortable with their abilities.

Legos are an amazing tool to get children building their own stories. Like blocks, Legos are structured in a way that invites children to become immersed in their imagination. The pieces allow them to build anything they set their minds to. These experiences are important not only for literacy in understanding story elements and characterization, but also for developing representational thinking. The children build representations of elements from their story. The representations do not look exactly what they might look like in the child's mind, or like the real thing if they are creating a familiar city building, and this is understood by the children when they enter a Lego experience. With this understanding, they are able to spend their cognitive energy on the story being created rather than on the details of the structures they are creating.

I did a workshop for the early childhood teachers at Catherine Cook that explored the links between Legos and literacy. Teachers should take the time to play with these tools to see the full potential for what they can provide for children. This video shows a pair of four-year-old children building elements of a story about Anansi the Spider.

After children have built their scenes, teachers can use an audio-recording resource such as Voice Recorder by Tapmedia to record the children sharing the story happening in the scene. This application allows users to export audio recordings as MP4 file formats, which can be uploaded to YouTube or Vimeo. Once uploaded, teachers can create QR codes to these links so visitors and other children can hear the stories. The application QR Reader by Tapmedia is a great tool for scanning and creating QR codes. Here is how a teacher displayed children's work and QR codes linked to recordings of their narratives.

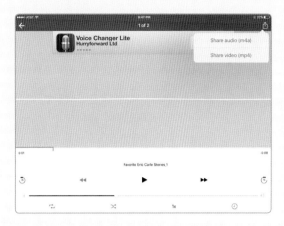

Supporting Learning: This type of experience has many valuable layers. First the students collaborated on the narrative they were going to create. They created their narratives, determining characters, setting, and plot. They decided who would build what out of which pieces. They negotiated who would use which space on the Lego baseplate. The many components to this activity offered valuable experiences that lasted for days. I visited this classroom on several consecutive days and found the children working in their groups, adding details to their structures.

Assessment and Documentation: As the children build their structures and develop their narratives, teachers can confer with the groups to learn more about how the process is going. You can ask questions such as these:

- How has your story changed since you started?
- Tell me about what you created here.
- Tell me what part each of you worked on.

Using the Collaborative Lego Experience Sheet (4.3) can be helpful in organizing the information you collect during these conversations and determining how to support the group.

4.3 Collaborative Lego Experience Sheet

Group members: Date:

Description of narrative:

How has your story changed since you started?

What have you created so far?

Tell me about the parts each of you worked on:

Plan for further support:

Sharing Learning with Others: The Voice Recorder and QR Reader applications make it very easy to share the collaborative work that is occurring. Visitors can scan the QR code to hear about the narrative, what has been created so far, and any future plans. When families have the ability to hear these conversations, they can get an idea of how the groups are collaborating to develop a story and create a Lego scene that matches the story.

Creating Podcasts to Share Classroom Events

Voice Recorder can be used for all sorts of experiences. Earlier I mentioned using the ComicBook! application to help children create newsletters. Voice Recorder can be a helpful resource to create podcasts that share classroom events. Children can share independently, in pairs, or in groups, depending on the content to be shared. For example, within a unit on travel, children could record a podcast that shares fun and exciting places to travel and why they think so. Additionally, the children could share the best way to travel there depending on the global geographical location. If the city of origin is Chicago and the destination is New Buffalo, Michigan, they may suggest a car or train; however, if they suggest Disney World in Florida, they may say to take a car or a train, but also include a plane.

In this experience, children use language and perhaps new vocabulary to discuss what is happening in the classroom. Moreover, children refine their ability to be articulate and understood by others, as they know an audience will be listening to the podcasts.

Remember that a child's podcast does not have to be long. A one-minute podcast can be loaded with information!

Supporting Learning: Creating and publishing podcasts provides children with another collaborative experience. They learn to work together to determine what to share, who will share what, and at what time. In the early stages of introducing this to children, teachers will need to help children in having these conversations successfully and productively. Over time they will learn how to share and negotiate the possible roles of creating and publishing a podcast.

Assessment and Documentation: As time goes by and the children are given some independence in the process of identifying their roles during planning and recording the podcast, teachers can keenly observe and listen to the conversations, identifying progression, growth, and increased ability to be independent in this collaborative process. In this observation, a teacher will learn who is developing these social skills and who needs some additional experiences to develop them.

Sharing Learning with Others: As mentioned earlier, once recordings are taken in the Voice Recorder application and then uploaded to a video hosting website such as YouTube or Vimeo, the audio recordings in these links can be shared with others. When this link is visited in any browser, individuals can listen to the recording. These podcasts can be shared via e-mail with the link included or via QR code on a poster or handout sent home.

Creating Newscast Shows

Children enjoy being in front of the camera. If a teacher has a class that is more likely to share information about classroom events through a video recording rather than an audio recording, the application TouchCast Studio is an easy tool to use. Teachers and children can choose a style of video with name captions and visuals that accompany the story, if they wish. These videos can be e-mailed and shared with other classrooms, other schools, and with families.

Supporting Learning: Similar to creating a podcast, TouchCast Studio allows children to share classroom happenings or important information and announcements with video rather than audio. When provided this option, children begin learning early that people can get information in all sorts of ways, such as via e-mail, video, live streaming, audio, paper mail, face-to-face, and sign language.

Assessment and Documentation: Children have different comfort levels and preferences as to how they share information and engage with people.

Some children enjoy drawing a picture and giving it to someone to show they care. Some children would rather sit and chat with someone for a period of time. When it comes to sharing information with an audience, some children will feel more comfortable sharing with an audio recording, whereas others would rather use video. Helping children recognize these preferences and comfort levels and then determining how to support them is important.

Sharing Learning with Others: TouchCast recordings can be shared; however, teachers should be aware that to e-mail them, their videos will have to be set to "public," making them viewable to anyone. If you are going to share them in that way, developing a release form for parents to sign, granting permission to turn on the public setting, is essential. Shared TouchCast Studio recordings give parents a glimpse into the classroom they would not otherwise be able to have. They would be able to see and hear straight from the students what is happening and what is about to happen in the weeks to come.

Creating Their Own Apps

Children are becoming more and more familiar with what an application is and where it can be accessed. They are learning that it can be a game, a collection of e-books, a place to draw and create, or a place to record words, sounds, or images. The application POP provides individuals with an opportunity to create a prototype of an application idea in development. Observed through an educational lens, this app allows children to enter the space of application creation with a developmentally appropriate approach. With the help of an adult or older child, a child imports photographs or illustrations into POP and then links the illustrations together by choosing "hot spots" on the image. These hot spots become the hyperlink, or link from one image to another image. In a kindergarten writer's workshop, children learn about writing how-to books. POP could be a resource for the children to share their knowledge and expertise in another way. For example, if a child has a particular interest in airplanes, with the help of an adult, the child could create an application that tells others about airplanes in the child's own words. The application can then be shared via e-mail with anyone using an Apple platform.

Scan the QR code here to take a look at how this is done:

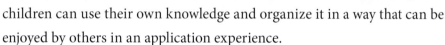

Or go to https://youtu.be/flUXlVQk5wA.

Supporting Learning: Children are seeing adults and other children use applications all the time. They are more than likely using apps themselves. Therefore, helping children understand the many ways we can use applications in our lives is essential. Young children typically see applications as games. In this experience, children can use their own knowledge and organize it in a way that can be enjoyed by others in an application experience.

Assessment and Documentation: As children determine how they want to organize the application, they will assign areas to put certain pieces of information. As children do this, the teacher can learn about each child's ability to organize information and utilize creativity to convey messages. As teachers learn these characteristics of the children in their class, they can determine moments when these skills can be used for the greater good of the classroom.

Sharing Learning with Others: The applications created in POP can be shared via e-mail with a URL link. They can be navigated in any browser and on most smartphones. Even though the applications are created in an iOS environment, they can be viewed and enjoyed in other environments. These applications can be shared with the other students in the class and with their families so they can learn from the student. Other classrooms might also be interested in seeing the application, as the creator is a similar age and the content might be a match in terms of interest.

Conclusion

Early childhood educators are on the lookout for experiences and tools that meet the individual literacy needs of children. Technology can be that tool when used at the right time. However, the application you are using on a multi-touch mobile device might not be originally intended for a literacy purpose. Teachers often wonder how, besides providing e-books, they can use technology to support young learners in the area of literacy. There are all sorts of ways, but finding them requires thinking outside the box.

Forms 4

4.1 Internet Features and Functions Record Sheet

www.redleafpress.org/techpk/4-1.pdf

4.2 Early Writer's Conference Sheet

www.redleafpress.org/techpk/4-2.pdf

4.3 Collaborative Lego Experience Sheet

www.redleafpress.org/techpk/4-3.pdf

4.1 Internet Features and Functions Record Sheet

Date:	Feature/function:	Revisit in near future:
		Yes / No
		Yes / No
		Yes / No
		Yes / No
		Yes / No
		Yes / No
		Yes / No

4.2 Early Writer's Conference Sheet

Child:	Date:	Content of conference:	Next step(s):

4.3 Collaborative Lego Experience Sheet

Group members: Date:

Description of narrative:

How has your story changed since you started?

What have you created so far?

Tell me about the parts each of you worked on:

Plan for further support:

Art 5

WHEN I WAS IN MIDDLE SCHOOL, I loved watching the television show *In Search Of*, narrated by Leonard Nimoy. *In Search Of* was a show that explored mysterious events or beings in history, most of which have various theories behind them to explain their existence. I was fascinated by the topics of investigation, such as Amelia Earhart, Bigfoot, the creation of the pyramids, the giant squid, and the *Titanic*. The story of the *Titanic* was quite interesting to me: I was intrigued by the size of the ship and astounded by the process of its sinking and breaking in two. I feared what it would have been like to be on board at the time of the sinking, and I wanted to hear what the survivors had to say. I continued my research, watched other videos and documentaries, and found books that provided more details, perspectives, and theories. While reading, I developed an interest in rebuilding or re-creating the *Titanic*. I found models, which I built. I also used my Lego bricks to re-create the ship. Finally, I turned to painting. I found that I was able to replicate the ship best with a brush. I painted the *Titanic* in several stages of the sinking process. Looking back on this entire experience, I am amazed at how the interest in a historical event led me to process it best through creative expression. The media helped me collect facts and information and develop more questions. I wonder how I would have processed this interest differently if I had had access to some of today's creative and artistic digital resources. Artists today have access to many other media. Perhaps I could have drawn a scene in the iPad application called Paper that would look just like a pen-and-ink drawing, but I would have had the ability to erase. I wonder what it would have been like to design the *Titanic* in Morphi and then print a 3D model of it in a MakerBot 3D printer.

I have heard many individuals say they believe that technology reduces children's ability to explore and develop their creativity, and then I hear them describe a scene of children sitting at a desktop computer playing games. However, if one is aware of the many resources, tools, and applications available, technology can be harnessed to nurture, support, and encourage creativity rather than reduce it. Such applications on multi-touch mobile devices provide children with the opportunity to tinker, explore, create, remix media, and share their ideas with their own creative expressions (Katz-Buonincontro and Foster 2013).

Bring Artwork to Life with Augmented Reality

As mentioned previously, augmented reality applications provide children with an opportunity to see and process concepts in an exciting experience. When working with art materials, young children enjoy seeing how fast they can turn a piece of paper orange by coloring with an orange marker or crayon. They are interested in seeing how many fringes they can put on a piece of paper by cutting into it with scissors. They guess how large they can make a mountain made of clay. When it comes to drawing, an application called Quiver allows children to bring their two-dimensional work to life in three dimensions. Peter H. Reynolds, author of *The Dot*, has instituted International Dot Day, which celebrates children making their mark on the world. It also celebrates children embracing their individuality. The Quiver application utilizes the built-in

> I am not normally an advocate for coloring sheets; however, this experience is unique and allows children to bring their artwork to life in a way that is not possible with any other resource.

camera on an iPad to capture and view illustrations made by children. Quiver has printable sheets that the children color. These printable sheets are necessary as the drawings on them contain intentional shapes and features that give the application information about how to bring the illustrations to life.

For Dot Day, Quiver created a sheet with a large open circle for children to create their own dots. When their dots are viewed in the application, they pop up off the page on the screen. The children are able to put their hands under the iPad, in view of the camera, making it look like they are holding the dots in their hands. Our younger artists illustrated dots and brought them to life. Art teacher Sandra Kane made a bulletin board with their dots posted along with a QR code to a link where parents and visitors could download the application. Then, right there, individuals could view the dots pop right off the bulletin board before their very eyes. This experience is like no other. Quiver has other sheets that could fit into popular areas of study. There is a dragon that can be illustrated, and when viewed, will fly up off the page and even blow fire. This could be part of an investigation around castles. There is a sheet with an airplane that artists can illustrate, and when viewed in the application, the airplane flies above the sheet through the clouds. This could be part of an investigation on transportation.

Supporting Learning: This experience invites children to create their own dots and bring them into a 3D experience. In doing so, children learn that art comes in many forms. Sometimes these forms are tangible, and sometimes they appear as if in a manufactured, alternate reality that we

cannot hold in our hands. This experience also helps children begin to appreciate the complexity of electronics and how this complexity can make pieces of artwork that had never been imagined before. As children see these possibilities early on, they become part of their creative fabric and integrated into their brainstorming and innovative thinking for years to come.

When the dots are viewed in the app, users can bring the dots into 3D in a few different ways, one of which looks like moons revolving around a planet. Consider using this same sheet again if your group enjoys exploring and researching planets. The children could create their own planets with moons revolving around them.

Assessment and Documentation: This experience allows for teachers to ask all sorts of questions to gather different pieces of information. Perhaps the teacher would like to know about how the students are processing the possibility of this phenomenon. Maybe the teacher would like the students to draw a certain type of scene of their dots, like a favorite vacation spot. The teacher would then ask questions based on that scene.

Sharing Learning with Others: As indicated earlier, Sandra Kane placed the dots on a bulletin board so that visitors and families could view the dots in a 3D experience. Providing individuals outside of the classroom with the same experience allows them to get an idea of how the children are learning that technology can support their art exploration and creativity.

Stop-Motion Videos with Clay and Paper

In chapter 3, I discussed using I Can Animate and iMotion HD to create stop-motion videos for children to record and share how they created block structures. Stop Motion Studio is another stop-motion video creation application. These same applications can be used to help children create stop-motion videos with all sorts of materials, from Legos to stuffed animals, clay, and paper. Children enjoy creating stories around their clay characters, and those who prefer paper do as well.

Depending on the content, stop-motion videos can take a good deal of time. You may want to take a few clips, take a break, and come back to it. Let the children take the lead and see how much time they would like to spend on it.

Once these videos are created using the time-lapsed photo approach, they can be imported into a movie-making application such as iMovie. In iMovie, children can insert a voice-over to narrate their stories. Depending on the artwork and characters created, the narration may need to be done in pairs or in small groups, making it a collaborative effort. This experience helps children develop patience and perseverance, as these projects can take time.

Scan here to see how Stop Motion Studio works:

Or go to www.youtube.com/watch?v=5C2LS81VA5Q.

Supporting Learning: Being an artist requires patience, understanding, a creative and critical eye, and perseverance. Developing a value for perseverance is an important goal in the early childhood setting. Creating a stop-motion video takes time, creative thinking, and a plan. In creating and recording these videos, children are able to experience perseverance in an activity that is driven by their plan and on their timeline. This provides an authentic and meaningful entry point to appreciating perseverance.

Assessment and Documentation: As teachers assist and observe a child or a small group of children determining their narrative to be told, the characters to be made and used, the frames to be shot, and the words to be spoken, they can collect a great deal of information about a child's developing capacity to persevere, particularly in a literacy and artwork context. Teachers can learn about the points with which children seem to have the most difficulty, when they seem to have the most success, and how they collaborate and advocate for their and others' ideas when it comes to problem solving.

Sharing Learning with Others: Depending on the size of the videos, they can be shared via e-mail with other classrooms and families. Another way is to have a small monitor by the pickup and drop-off area with some of these videos looping without audio. Have a

At some point, try omitting audio with the videos, and as the students watch the videos, invite them to add their own dialogue between the characters, creating their own narrative. It is interesting to see what the children come up with.

whiteboard adjacent to the monitor and invite families to watch them and jot down what they think the videos are about. This information will be exciting and more than likely surprising to the young filmmakers.

Drawing and 3D Printing

Art centers in early childhood classrooms provide children with experience to practice and develop new technical art skills using materials such as scissors, glue, and clay, as well as exploring other materials such as by folding, crinkling, and rolling paper (Dinnerstein 2016). As the access to emerging technology tools expands, 3D printers have been added to the long list of opportunities. The maker movement has become increasingly popular in school settings over the past five years, particularly in the upper elementary, middle, and secondary grades. These spaces are intended to help children create structures, machines, and art with a plan in mind. This approach is not at all new to early childhood. Young children have always been making things; it's a significant way in which they learn and interact with the world.

Emily, my daughter's mom, has a sewing machine at her house and loves making things for family members. After she finishes one of these projects, she usually has quite a bit of scrap fabric left over. When I was teaching, I would bring these bags of fabric into class and discuss them in our morning meeting. We would talk about what we could do with them. I vividly remember the art center turning into a fashion studio as children began making their own clothes. There were skirts, shirts, bracelets, hats, and much more. The imagination and innovation were quite inspiring. We even held a fashion show at one point. Children love to take materials and create something new.

Within this maker movement has come the use of 3D printers, machines of varying size that use a plastic filament to print a three-dimensional object. Of course, 3D printers come at varying price points, the expensive ones having the better printed result. The software used to design items to be 3D printed has for a long time been inaccessible to young children. Now, however, the Doodle 3D Wi-Fi box makes it possible for children to design and then export that design to a 3D printer for printing. This box acts as a middleman between a sleek and easy-to-use drawing program and the 3D printer. Children can visit a website on a computer, laptop, iPhone, iPad, or other device, design and draw, and simply hit Print. The Wi-Fi box wirelessly receives the drawing and sends it to the 3D printer to begin printing. As children have experiences with 3D printing, they experience a strong sense of agency, while at the same time develop skills that are necessary for thoughtful design (Thornburg, Thornburg, and Armstrong 2014).

Doodle 3D Wi-Fi Box

Scan here to learn more about the Doodle 3D Wi-Fi box:

Or go to https://youtu.be/8p2QGWlhR4E.

Wondering where to find a 3D printer that you can use temporarily because you cannot afford to buy one? Call your local public library to get more information. In communities where these resources are not in schools, libraries and media centers are beginning to acquire them for the community. If you know of a school that does have one, give them a call and see if they would be open to you coming in and taking a look. Most schools are interested in building relationships with other schools and organizations in the community.

This can be a valuable experience for children to bring their artwork to life for various purposes. Consider these examples of when a child might want to 3D print their design:

- create a unique stencil for drawing

- create an ornament as a gift

- create a stick puppet for a dramatic play center

- design a particular block needed in the block center

- produce a figurine of a character from a favorite story

When children are provided these opportunities, they can see their designs go from thoughts on paper to tangible objects ready to be used for the intended purpose. The ability for this to happen provides children with a higher level of investment in their own exploration while developing creativity, problem solving, and artistic thinking.

Supporting Learning: These experiences are necessary for young children to help them develop an innovative, creative, and confident mind-set when it comes to art and design. The art centers in classrooms offer a world of opportunities, but there are many more with materials that have not traditionally been found in classrooms. As children are provided with a learning environment that invites experimentation and an opportunity to develop creativity through trial and error, they build confidence and a voice through art expression.

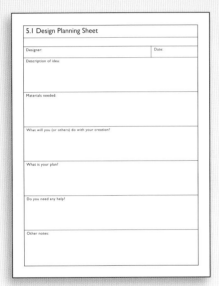

Assessment and Documentation: Consider using the Design Planning Sheet (5.1) to help the children create their plan and bring it to fruition, from sketch to a sculpture or 3D print. This sheet will help teachers gather information not only about the plan but where the idea came from and how the children's creation will be used once it is finished.

Sharing Learning with Others: As indicated, the Design Planning Sheet (5.1) will collect a substantial amount of information regarding the children's ideas and plans. As the children work through their plans, collect work samples along the way. The children may not finish in one, two, or even three days. Because young children are developing a sense of perseverance, having all the materials ready to go when they intend to resume their work is crucial. Not only will having these items be helpful for the children in their design execution, but they will also make for authentic pieces for discussion in a parent-teacher conference. When children have finished making artwork, showcasing it in a way that shows it is being valued is imperative. Consider these possible ways of showcasing children's artwork:

- taking photographs and displaying on a bulletin board

- framing drawings and paintings

- displaying 3D objects on small risers or pedestals

- sharing a photo gallery online

- having an art gallery showing every other month

- featuring a classroom artist with an interview and some of the artist's favorite creations

Creating 3D Objects with Paper

Children enjoy working with scissors, tape, and paper. Watching them create something remarkable is quite fascinating. When I was teaching, we did an author study on Mo Willems. To go along with his series of pigeon books, we made a bulletin board with pigeons all over it with speech bubbles for each one. The class made their own pigeons and speech bubbles. The sizes, proportions, and levels of detail were valuable information for me to determine where the children were in their fine-motor skills, hand-eye coordination, problem solving, and creativity.

I have discovered many opportunities to support children's fine motor skills, some that begin with a digital entry point. Foldify is an application where children can illustrate on templates that can be printed out and then cut out and folded into a particular shape. Some of the possible creations include a cube, a rectangular prism, a pyramid, a car, and a house.

Scan here to take a peek at what it looks like:

Or go to https://youtu.be/j-1j_oc7HF8.

Consider the following ideas.

Writer's Block

In kindergarten, children often get introduced to the idea of writer's workshop. Part of the launch of this process includes creating some device for children to refer to for ideas to write about. I have seen a "writer's heart" where the writers include a list or images of things that are important to them. They could also create a "writer's block" with illustrations of people, places, or things that are interesting, exciting, or meaningful to them.

Create a Character from a Story

Children enjoy acting out stories with puppets or props. Foldify can help them create paper characters for story retelling.

Create a Car for the Block Center

Structures built in the block center often include ramps, garages, and secret passages. If Legos are not available, or if a child would prefer, the application provides sheets that can be printed, illustrated, cut out, and then folded into the shape of a car or truck. Once completed, they could be included in the play with the structure.

Family Cube

At the beginning of the school year, as part of the community-building efforts, children often share about their family members, what they do, and what is important to them. Children can create a cube illustrating these elements. Young children can also find it frightening to share or speak in front of a group, so having the cube with them while they share can be a helpful reminder of what they wanted to share.

Feelings Cube

Depending on the shape chosen, children will require support in cutting out the Foldify templates they illustrate.

Throughout the early years, children are learning about feelings and emotions. While doing so, they also learn about empathy and sympathy. This can be difficult for children, particularly when they are focused on articulating how they feel. Too often children are only taught very basic feelings: mad, sad, angry, and happy. To help the children explore other feelings, such as shocked, curious, and irritated, you may want to encourage some children to create a feelings cube that gives them a visual and textual cue for feelings they may be experiencing. This cube can be used when they are having a social problem-solving conversation with another child or adult.

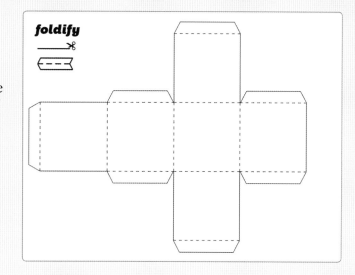

In these experiences, the children explore a whole host of skills while being creative. They develop fine-motor skills, they explore social-emotional vocabulary, and they use strategies to help them move forward when they feel stuck. Creativity through art is a vehicle to explore and develop other important skills.

Supporting Learning: Before preschool and kindergarten, many children's encounter with art is limited to drawing on paper.

This experience involves children designing all sorts of 3D objects out of folded paper. Young designers can create robots, cars, blocks, and more. This is a perfect opportunity to introduce the careful use of scissors as the children cut out their patterns to be folded. The open-ended approach to these designs invites teachers to think outside the box. Consider the example of having kindergartners create writer's blocks. Here their artwork is supporting the growth in another subject area.

Assessment and Documentation: A variety of examples are provided with which teachers could approach an application like this. Consider using the 3D Cube Planning Sheet (5.2) to help the children plan out what will go on each side of the cube as they illustrate it in the application. Later a teacher can cross-reference the plan with what the children actually drew, determining if they carried out their plan or not. For example, if a child was going to make a feelings cube and indicated that he was going to make a cube of different happy faces, but when reviewing the cube, the teacher notices it is a variety of sad

While this two-dimensional art experience is valuable, teachers need to expose children to many opportunities to create three-dimensional art. The previous strategy discussed was 3D printing. Consider allowing children to work with wood to design houses. Allow the students to glue these pieces together. If your program is on a strict budget, invite family members to donate small pieces of wood and craft sticks.

faces, the teacher can have a conversation with the child about emotions, feelings, and facial expressions to see if there are any misconceptions that need to be addressed.

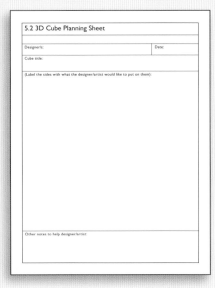

Sharing Learning with Others:

When children have made their 3D Foldify art, they find creative ways to showcase their work. Perhaps place them on a windowsill or on a bookshelf in the reading corner, affix them to a bulletin board, or place them on top of the children's cubbies. This way they can be enjoyed not only by the children in the class but also by visitors and families.

Observe your group's ability to hold markers and pens and their "finger-painting" on the screen. Depending on how the children handle these experiences, it might be helpful to obtain a stylus for them to use when drawing their designs in the Foldify application.

Light Up Those Drawings!

Children often feel extremely proud of their drawings. This is exhibited when they come running while announcing, "Look at what I made!" It is at this point that the artists begin explaining the story behind what they have drawn. Sticky circuits can help children add another layer to their drawings. Sticky circuits use copper tape, lights, and sensors to create unique features of the drawing on paper. If a child has drawn a robot, sensors can be added to the drawing that cause a light to go on when a button is pushed. These lights can help personalize characters the children have drawn or light up a room if they drew their house. These illustrations can be displayed on a bulletin board and help viewers understand a bit deeper what the artist had in mind.

Materials for these circuits can be purchased in packs through Chibitronics.com, individually on Amazon.com, or occasionally at local hardware and hobby stores. Do not be afraid to tell the hardware store employees what your plan is—they are helpful people! Do not just guess what you think you might need.

Scan here to take a closer look and learn more about how these simple circuits work:

Or go to https://youtu.be/LIwUU9TuVSU.

Supporting Learning: In this experience, children see how they can include simple circuits into their artwork. As mentioned in the discussion about the Quiver application, children can begin to understand how electronics wedded to art can create something new and inspiring. Young children enjoy drawing and sketching with crayons, markers, pencils, and chalk. If teachers provide children with the opportunity to include simple circuits into their illustrations, their ideas for what can be drawn and portrayed on paper can expand.

Assessment and Documentation: As the children brainstorm new ideas for incorporating the circuits into their illustrations, the teacher can learn about how children are approaching the novel concept of electronics and art. The teacher will learn about whether they see the circuit as energy making the light turn on, or perhaps they are still at a more primitive mind-set, thinking it is simply magic that makes the light go on. Either way, both pieces of information are important for the teacher to consider when developing future experiences for the group.

Sharing Learning with Others: Consider placing the children's drawings on a bulletin board where visitors and other classrooms can see the artwork light up. Or invite other classes to visit the classroom with the lights out and allow the children to try out the circuits. They will see the artwork light up the classroom.

Bringing Characters to Life with Animation

Many young children enjoy cartoons or animated shows. Today's technology offers this age group the opportunity to explore and try out animation themselves in a developmentally appropriate experience. ChatterPix is an application that invites users to animate characters' mouths with a recording of their own voices. Preschoolers are naturally curious about bugs and insects. Children illustrate a bug or insect they have seen and then animate their bug, perhaps telling where the bug may be going or what it wants to eat. Creating self-portraits is a typical developmental assessment for children in preschool

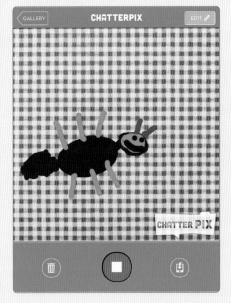

and kindergarten. After drawing a self-portrait, children can animate their illustrations by applying their own voices to the pictures by telling a few pieces of information about themselves.

Supporting Learning: In both of these experiences, young children are able to experience an authentic participation in animation. The animation may be still, with the exception of the mouth, but it is a developmentally appropriate entry point to the concept. Children need to learn that there are a variety of ways to express and share ideas through art. The way in which individuals can share these ideas looks different at various ages. The application ChatterPix literally provides the children's artwork with their own voices.

Assessment and Documentation: In both of these experiences, teachers as well as parents can learn a significant amount about what a child is learning. As children learn about bugs and insects, videos created in ChatterPix with their illustrations provide the opportunity for children to share what they have learned in terms of what bugs and insects do, what they need, and how they live their lives. In the use of ChatterPix with the self-portraits, children are able to share the following:

- information regarding the importance of certain body parts

- the narrative around what is happening in the illustration

- information regarding what they have learned since the beginning of the year

- characteristics or traits that are unique to themselves

This information can be used to communicate with parents and learning resources teachers at the school or setting.

Sharing Learning with Others: The videos created in the application can be saved within the application and exported to the device's collection of photos. Once in the photos, the video can be e-mailed; uploaded to YouTube,

Vimeo, or a digital portfolio resource such as Seesaw; texted; or uploaded to a social media network.

Scan the QR code to take a closer look at what ChatterPix has to offer:

 Or go to www.youtube.com/watch?v=_Iom-DiDIc8.

Enhancing the Art Gallery

It is common for schools and early childhood centers to include spaces where children's artwork is displayed. Typically, the artwork is matted and displayed with a small badge with the child's name, age, and classroom. Like the art galleries of the past, visitors are left to wonder what the artist had in mind when he created his work. However, today in art galleries, we see people walking around with headphones or audio devices that provide another layer of information about the work. When museum goers visit a piece of artwork, they can punch in a number related to the work and hear a detailed account of the artist's background, a historical quote from the artist, or perhaps a description of the inspiration for the work. Something similar can be done for young artists in early childhood settings.

Teachers can use Voice Recorder, mentioned earlier, as a quick and easy way to record the artists discussing their work. Depending on the child's vocabulary and ability to articulate, a child could discuss any of the following:

- name
- age
- grade/classroom
- what she made
- how she made it
- materials used

- why she made it

- where the idea came from

- what she might make next

- where to find her in the school/center if the viewer has questions

Remember to take a picture of the artist so viewers can feel like they are getting to know the artist, and may later recognize the artist around the school or center.

For early childhood educators to see young children as competent individuals is vital. It is true that they are learning and refining skills, but acknowledging the efforts and successes they have had will strengthen their confidence and willingness to try new things. In enhancing the art gallery experience in this way, teachers honor the work of young children just as communities honor the artists in the galleries. Seeing their work displayed as prominently as the work of famous artists in the museums is a powerful experience for children.

Supporting Learning: As children go around and listen to the other students describe their process, inspiration, or materials list, they will undoubtedly learn something from their fellow artists. This helps nurture the idea of sharing and collaboration. Artists learn from each other and help each other become better at their craft.

Consider enlisting parent volunteers to help with taking the recordings. They may also be helpful when it comes to scanning the QR codes so that the students can listen to them during the gallery walk. Use what you know about your group to determine the best way for the children to participate in the gallery showing and how they can access what their peers had to say about their work.

Assessment and Documentation: As the teacher listens to the children describe their inspirations, articulate their processes, and share plans for future artwork, the teacher can learn valuable information about how the children are able to use art supplies to create an image that displays a scene. The teacher is also able to learn about the developing confidence of the children and how they see themselves as artists. Knowing this information will be helpful in determining what materials to introduce next and what subject areas to introduce new art experiences in next.

Sharing Learning with Others: The structure and nature of this experience is for children to share what they learned through their creative process and what their next steps are as artists. The QR codes allow for anyone to listen at any time to the children describe and articulate. For family members not able to come in and view the gallery, consider sending home a handout with images of the artwork and the corresponding QR code next to it. This way family members unable to attend can listen in as well.

Exploring Digital Design and Building

Building and construction are often topics of high interest for young children. When teachers follow children's lead in terms of planning for learning, it is common to see units around building, skyscrapers, construction, and related materials emerge. At Catherine Cook, we recognize this interest and have been building a unit exploring construction. Here are a couple of the essential understandings within this unit:

- Buildings (towers and houses) can be constructed with a variety of materials.

- Towers are built in a certain way so they can remain standing tall.

The children are provided opportunities to build with all sorts of materials, such as various-sized blocks, Legos, wood planks, and craft sticks. We also introduce the idea of digital building. While we can design on paper with blueprints and then build based on our design, we can also build digitally in various software and applications. Blokify is designed in such a way that it provides children with a developmentally appropriate entry point to designing their own skyscrapers. Once completed, their designs are then sent to our 3D printers, where the children can hold their designs in the palms of their hands. Their prints are brought back to the classroom and incorporated into the block center.

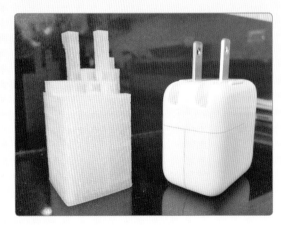

If a 3D printer is not accessible, Blokify offers the opportunity to send in designs to be 3D printed remotely. The prints are then sent to the artists via USPS.

Scan this QR code to learn more about Blokify:

Or go to https://youtu.be/3HW11u12z6w.

Supporting Learning: This experience helps children learn that designing can be done using a variety of tools and resources, both tangible and intangible. As educators of an evolving world with countless resources at our fingertips, we need to consider these resources in how we help children conceptualize and how we can nurture creative expression. The exposure to these resources will help children establish a foundation of what is possible in terms of creativity, construction, and design.

Assessment and Documentation: As children construct their towers, teachers can observe how the children incorporate concepts regarding construction. For example, one of the building concepts that may be taught in such a unit might be that a tower begins with a wider base to keep it sturdy. A teacher can introduce this concept in a variety of ways, perhaps in a children's book, by observing photographs or videos of familiar buildings in the neighborhood, and in a block center while building. While the children design their towers in Blokify, it is important to observe whether this same concept is incorporated in their tower designs.

Sharing Learning with Others: As mentioned, Blokify provides the ability to create 3D print designs. If a 3D printer is accessible or if the designs were sent in for printing, the designs and prints can be displayed in the classroom. Consider these examples for sharing their designs:

- Print screenshots of the design in Blokify and post next to the printed tower.

- Use Doodlecast Pro to compile screenshots of the designs with children describing their designs and why they designed them the way they did.

- Print screenshots of the designs in Blokify with a QR code linked to an audio or video clip of the children describing design.

- Record videos of children comparing block-based tower designs and the digitally designed towers.

Conclusion

Partners at IDEO, Tom and David Kelley, are also authors of *Creative Confidence: Unleashing the Creative Potential within Us All* (2013). They discuss the importance of embracing your own creativity. It is when we embrace our own creativity, leaving aside the fears of what others will think of our ideas and trials, that we discover a pasture of opportunity—opportunity to think further outside of the box than we ever thought imaginable. Teachers often become bogged down with the day-to-day routines and mandates. They slowly realize they feel stripped of their creative side. Teachers need to hold tight to what makes them creative, enthusiastic, and eager to work with children and families. They need to keep their creativity secure and valued, and share it with the children with whom they work. In doing so, they nurture the creative spirit that children want and need. An easy place to start doing this is with art.

5 Forms

5.1 Design Planning Sheet

www.redleafpress.org/techpk/5-1.pdf

5.2 3D Cube Planning Sheet

www.redleafpress.org/techpk/5-2.pdf

5.1 Design Planning Sheet

Designer:	Date:

Description of idea:

Materials needed:

What will you (or others) do with your creation?

What is your plan?

Do you need any help?

Other notes:

5.2 3D Cube Planning Sheet

Designer/s:	Date:

Cube title:

(Label the sides with what the designer/artist would like to put on them):

foldify

Other notes to help designer/artist:

Music | 6

YOUNG CHILDREN SEEM TO NATURALLY enjoy music. I often listen to Pandora, an Internet radio service by which subscribers can choose artists they like and a station is generated with music by artists in that same genre. As individuals listen, they can "like" songs, which will then change the station song list, adding more songs by that particular artist. Teachers have begun using this service in their classrooms to set a particular mood during self-selected center time, or perhaps during writer's workshop. I can remember my daughter, Lydia, beginning to bounce her body around to the beats of our music when she was around six months old. I remember my nieces and nephew doing the same thing at around that age. Their sense of pride in the accomplishment is something I will never forget. As Lydia has gotten older, her dance moves have evolved, such as adding raised hands in the air and swaying side to side. As our technology continues to evolve, so do the ways in which we can invite children to explore and enjoy the world of music.

Creating and Mixing Music

When considering materials and resources for a music center, including music from a variety of cultures and genres is important (Isbell and Yoshizawa 2016). ButtonBass is an application-based and online-based resource that allows children to mix music by simply touching keys on a keyboard or tapping cubes on an iPad. ButtonBass offers a variety of genres online, providing children with the opportunity to explore mixing music within a variety of interests. Children are not often given the opportunity to experience electronic music. This and the following resources provide a developmentally appropriate entry point to exploring various genres by not only listening but also composing.

Scan the QR code here to see ButtonBass in action:

Or to to https://youtu.be/GMSS8uMTs8U.

Keezy is an easy-to-use app that allows users to mix music together with provided sounds and their own imported sounds. This application would be very useful in helping children listen to and then replicate a steady beat, as users are in charge of when sounds are applied.

Scan the QR code here for a quick look at how Keezy works:

Or go to www.youtube.com/watch?v=tbAiMxo76FI.

Scan the QR code here to observe a demonstration of a few more-complex ways to use Keezy:

Or go to https://www.youtube.com /watch?v=d38jQzOgPNU.

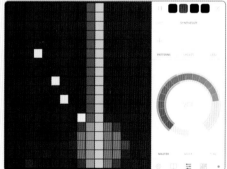

Beatwave is an application that offers a unique musical experience while offering teachers opportunities to explore more sophisticated mixing. In this application, children touch a box that has a unique note, different from all the other squares. A bar moves across the grid, playing the selected sound as it passes it. As children touch more squares, it plays them as well, changing the overall sound of the sequence. Children can add multiple layers to add different sounds. For example, one layer might be a drum and another layer might be a piano. Beatwave has a wide range of features, providing the opportunity to create simple or very sophisticated instrumental songs, as well as mixed tracks and compilations.

Scan here to see Beatwave in action:

Or go to https://www.youtube.com /watch?v=ckYsYCIqrFw.

Children can use this application to explore the different sounds made by different instruments, explore how to mix instrument sounds together to create unique instrumental (non-lyrical) music, identify high and low sounds, and of course, explore their musical creativity. The depth and complexity to which the child delves into these musical activities will be determined by

- the specific goals the teacher has for the experience,

- what the child can do independently,

Because Beatwave can appear to be a complex application, carrying out a slow and thoughtful introduction is imperative. Then the children will be more successful in maximizing the possibilities of this software. It is okay for children to need a steady stream of support while engaging with this application. Remember that independence is not paramount; it's the experience that is important.

- the child's interest in the experience, and
- available buddy or adult support.

Supporting Learning: This application allows children to explore a whole host of skills and concepts within music. Beyond the musical skill development, children can be provided an opportunity to cocompose and create music. They can work together to identify the sounds to add and then listen to their creation to determine if they think their composition is a success. Independently or with a teacher, the children can go back in to add or subtract sounds to achieve desired sounds or effects. These experiences are essential for children to engage with, as they provide children with an idea of how established musical artists collaborate. In a studio, artists will listen together to identify certain points in a song that need editing or changes.

Assessment and Documentation: As teachers observe children collaborating on their mixes, they can jot down notes regarding the children's ability to listen carefully and identify areas for change. They can also make notes regarding the children's ability to work together and to negotiate changes to the track, as well as their ability to mix sounds together.

Sharing Learning with Others: The mixes made by the children can be shared in a variety of ways. They can be uploaded to SoundCloud (an audio file hosting website), Twitter, or Facebook, and can also be e-mailed. Another feature allows the musical artists to import their mixes directly into iMovie. Children can overlay their own mixes on slideshows or videos they have taken. This provides a whole new avenue for creativity and creation with their mixes. When these mixes are shared with family members, followers on Twitter, or Facebook friends, listeners can gain a sense of how the children are approaching music—electronic music in particular—and how they are able to utilize their own creativity to create and share new tracks.

DJ Mix Kids Pro is an application that brings young children as close as they can get to being a live mixing deejay with the music they may know and love. A significant part of a high-quality early childhood program or curricular approach includes opportunities to learn through play. As teachers plan experiences for young children to learn new skills and concepts, they think intentionally about how play can take a core role in that development. Dramatic play experiences offer children opportunities try on the roles of others. Some dramatic play centers are a kitchen, a library, a post office, a castle, or a pet store. In this play, children take on other people's perspectives, take turns, create stories, and solve problems, and they can also create music. As a way to open up the world of possibilities with music, teachers can bring instruments and

music-making devices into the dramatic play center. Consider creating a deejay booth or music stage. In this experience, children can try on the perspective of a performer. These individuals, however, can be performing in different ways—playing an instrument, singing a song, or mixing music electronically. Deejays of all kinds use their musical skills to add their own creative touch to sounds and music. The application DJ Mix Kids Pro invites children to become a deejay and add beats and sounds to familiar sounds. These recordings can be recorded and shared via e-mail. This application on an iPad can add another area of creativity for children visiting this center to explore. This application is structured in a way that makes it easy to navigate. After a simple introduction to the application, many children are able to mix their own music independently or with a friend.

Scan the QR code here to take a look at how DJ Mix Kids Pro works:

Or go to www.youtube.com/watch?v=dwkHJ7ZZItA.

Incredibox is another resource that invites users to mix music. Unlike DJ Mix Kids Pro, Incredibox does have some voices and lyrics that can be added to the mixes. Incredibox provides a variety of beats, effects, voices, and chorus options to mix together. Users can decide when and for how long a sound is part of the mix. Any sound can be turned off at any time. Take a look at this

These experiences provide children with the opportunity to establish a foundation for a unique skill and art of mixing music. Identifying this interest early on helps children develop their identity as artists and individuals and provides a possible sense of direction to take in pursuing interests outside of the standard curriculum. For example, at Catherine Cook I offer a morning elective to middle school students that invites children to continue exploring their interest in deejaying and electronic music with professional mixing gear.

mix that I made for our Catherine Cook families just before we went on spring break.

Scan the QR code here to watch this mix in action:

Or go to http://bit.ly/1guDsko.

Scan the QR code here to observe a demonstration on the creation of these mixes:

Or go to www.youtube.com/watch?v=QUvkkqA9os0.

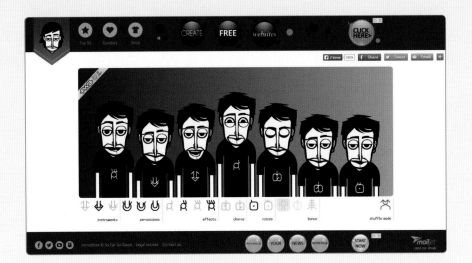

To help children stay on beat, show them how to count to three in their minds. If that is too difficult for some, try having them say a word three times in their minds. For example, "Say 'cup' three times, then make your noise, and keep doing that over and over."

Incredibox has four different styles of music to choose from, one of which is sounds made by individuals rather than instruments. When trying this one, discuss how each person makes his sound at the exact same moment every time. After the children seem to understand that concept, invite them to try it on their own with a group of other children. Each child can come up with his own sound to make, and a child can choose to be the one who decides when each child makes his sound, just as a conductor would. In this experience, children are able to see synchronized music modeled while they are in charge of it. Having this modeled for them on the website, children move off the computer and try it on their own with their own invented sounds. The experience of moving off the computer is important so that the children begin to recognize the role of being part of a group, staying on beat, listening to the other sounds, and following the instructions of the conductor.

Scan here to take a look:

Or go to www.youtube.com/watch?v=fTQgbHkblqY.

Visit www.incredibox.com on a computer to try it out. This resource cannot be used on multi-touch mobile devices as it requires Adobe Flash Player to operate it unless the Puffin Browser application is installed.

Supporting Learning: Like Beatwave, this resource invites children to explore the possibilities of collaboratively mixing music. The characters and color-coded costumes make it easy for children to identify what the characters will do when a certain costume is applied. This resource makes it easy for children to see how ensembles operate in an effort that considers consistency and timing. Many young children begin participating in school assemblies by singing songs and playing simple instruments such as bells and xylophones. Having an experience in Incredibox can help children observe and understand the importance of listening and timing. In DJ Mix Kids Pro, children have the opportunity to quickly and easily select a sound or instrument to be added to a familiar nursery rhyme.

Assessment and Documentation: Teachers can observe how the children interact and engage with each other as they collaborate to create a mix. These novel experiences offer teachers an opportunity to assess how the children are developing social-emotional skills such as turn taking, listening, and advocating for one's idea. In terms of music skill, teachers can listen in on the changes and edits each child recommends. These edits and changes can provide the teacher with valuable information regarding the children's ability to apply new skills and concepts

6.1 Music Mixing Record Sheet	
Name/s:	Date:
Describe child's ability to take turns:	
Describe child's ability to advocate for his or her own ideas:	
Next steps for child:	

Beatwave, DJ Mix Kids Pro, and Incredibox offer opportunities for children to mix music. After reviewing these resources, you will see that they are different in terms of complexity. In a large-group context, consider introducing DJ Mix Kids Pro first, Incredibox second, and Beatwave third. However, individuals or small groups of children might benefit more from one over the other at different times. Pay close attention to how the students are engaging with these resources to determine the best one to use at a given time.

in music. For example, perhaps one child identifies that the volume of one part of the track is too loud and needs to be lowered to be more appreciated by listeners. Consider using the Music Mixing Record Sheet (6.1) to help you document the collaborative experience.

Sharing Learning with Others: Both DJ Mix Kids Pro and Incredibox provide opportunities for the musicians to share their creations. In the classroom context, e-mail would likely be the easiest way to share the created tracks. As family members, friends, and followers listen to the mixes, they can get a better idea of how the children are considering how instruments and sound can be intentionally integrated into existing songs or songs created from scratch. Hearing these tracks will also help listeners learn more about how the children are exploring and embracing their developing creativity within music and sound.

Programming and Music

Wonder Workshop, the overarching name for the two companion robots Dash and Dot, offer children unique ways to explore math and music simultaneously. Dash, a programmable robot that can move around on a tripod, has all sorts of

functions. One of the functions includes the ability to program Dash to play a xylophone via an iPad application. Through simple directional commands, a child can determine how to program Dash to play certain colored bars. A kindergartner could have a simple piece of sheet music with colored bars indicating certain notes and program Dash to play the song.

Supporting Learning: In this experience, through a visual, non-textual approach, children can utilize their ability to count forward and backward (between one and ten) to program Dash to play a certain song. Teachers are always on the lookout for strategies and experiences where they can observe children employing new skills in an authentic context.

Assessment and Documentation: As children program Dash to play, teachers can observe how the children apply their developing capabilities to use numeracy and sequencing to achieve a particular result. Consider using the Xylophone Program Record Sheet (6.2) to document the experiences for children programming Dash. This sheet will be helpful in articulating the children's ability to apply new math concepts to supporting teachers and parents. It will also provide the teacher with a valuable artifact exhibiting how the child is able to use the strategy in an authentic context.

Sharing Learning with Others: This experience can be shared by recording it in a variety of ways. Teachers can record the experience on video using the camera on a multi-touch mobile device application. It can also be recorded using a simple digital voice recorder. The video or digital audio file can then be shared via e-mail, Vimeo, or YouTube. As individuals view the videos or listen to the recordings, they can get a better idea of how the children are considering music as a medium to further explore creativity and mathematics. Screenshots of the program developed by the musician could also be images that teachers might consider sharing via e-mail or a classroom website to show another part of the process of arriving at Dash playing the xylophone.

Scan here to see a demonstration on how to make music using the xylophone accessory for Dash the robot:

Programming Dash to play the xylophone is a way to integrate math and music in a very tangible and explicit fashion for young children. These experiences are not intended to replace children holding mallets and playing the xylophone themselves.

Or go to www.youtube.com/watch?v=DTO-hbcsuW4.

Using Makey Makey to Support Exploration

Making, tinkering, and engineering should be elements of any classroom. These approaches can also be present in experiences exploring concepts in music. Understanding the difference between the three, however, is important. In the book *Invent to Learn: Making, Tinkering, and Engineering in the Classroom*, authors Sylvia Libow Martinez and Gary Stager say very eloquently that "making" is the active and important role that construction plays while learning (2013). Young children have always been making, and they seem to have this natural sense and drive to use materials to create something new. "Tinkering" is a state of mind or an approach to thinking. It involves embracing experimentation and discovery. "Engineering" is a bit more complex. It involves synthesizing knowledge about the social world, being creative, and understanding global needs and using them to inform design and invention. Makey Makey allows anyone to turn everyday materials—such as a banana, wet paper towel, or glass of water—into instruments.

Supporting Learning: Utilizing Makey Makey as a tool for exploring music opens doors for children to use nontraditional materials as instruments. My daughter loves water. I used Makey Makey with small dishes of water, an apple, and an apricot, and together we played a piano on my laptop. Young children enjoy time at a sand and water table, where they can explore cause and effect with various materials. They are captured by observing how sand, water, or rice descending down a suspended wheel ends up back at the bottom. Makey Makey provides children with another way to explore what can happen with these everyday materials. More important, it provides them with an opportunity to see what can happen when they are in charge of these materials.

Assessment and Documentation: Similar to with using Wonder Workshop, teachers can record these musical moments using a variety of video and recording applications and devices. Teachers may consider using a tripod to record the entire experience on video. As teachers review these recordings and observe children interacting with these everyday materials to create music, they can learn about how the children can relate these nontraditional instruments to instruments with which they are familiar. For example, a teacher could ask, "How is this apricot similar to using a mallet on a drum?" The answer to a question such as this would provide the teacher with information about how the children are able to apply new musical concepts to novel experiences and materials that are not traditional instruments.

Sharing Learning with Others: Sharing these recordings, whether video or audio, would help families see not only how music is valued in the curriculum, but also how the children are applying their skills and concepts in a new context. Having the opportunity to view these videos or listen to the tracks could also help families think outside the box in terms of using household materials as nontraditional instruments as well, thus providing their children with an additional opportunity and experience to employ these new skills.

Scan the QR code here to take a closer look at Makey Makey:

Or go to www.youtube.com/watch?v=rfQqh7iCcOU.

Patatap as an Entry Point to Music

Patatap is an animation and sound kit in the form of an iPhone/iPad application and web-based resource found at www.patatap.com. This resource uses any desktop computer or laptop computer keyboard as the music keyboard. When a child strikes a key on the keyboard, a short animation and sound will appear on the screen. If the child presses multiple keys simultaneously, she will see and hear the sounds integrated together, showing an interesting display of animations along with a compilation of a variety of sounds. The iPhone/

iPad application does not require a keyboard but considers the specific place that you put your finger down on the screen to determine what animation and sound will appear.

Scan the QR code to take a look at an example of this resource in action:

Or go to www.youtube.com/watch?v=Sdj5Zge9wGM.

Supporting Learning: This application and web-based resource can help children explore music and art in a simple and explicit experience. Their one touch on the keyboard or interface provides them with two modes of response, visual and auditory. Young children are also exploring cause and effect in all sorts of experiences: at the sand and water table as they pour the water on the floor, at lunch as they smash their apple into their sandwich, on the playground as they toss the ball as far as they can. In this experience, they can see and hear what happens musically when they interact with a tool with the touch of a finger.

Assessment and Documentation: Patatap requires children to listen and consider timing when they press certain keys or touch a certain place on the multi-touch mobile device. Teachers can observe the children creating sounds and look for consistency and repetition. For example, if using the website version of Patatap, they can touch the A key on the keyboard, then B, and then C, and then repeat that same sequence at the same tempo to attempt to achieve a rhythmic sound with these keys. Children who are able to do this may be ready to include another key (sound effect) in their creation. Maintaining a tempo in the context of this resource requires skill. A hand over hand approach can be helpful to demonstrate what a maintained sequence and tempo can sound like.

Sharing Learning with Others: At this time, Patatap does not have a recording feature. Consider using a video camera on a multi-touch mobile device or a camcorder to capture the experience. The visuals are important in this experience, so I recommend using a video-recording strategy rather than just an audio-recording solution. Children can share their sequences by projecting the multi-touch mobile device, computer, or laptop on a screen using an LCD projector. This way, the entire group can see the animations and hear the sounds. To incorporate an element of literacy, consider inviting the children to "play" their first names. Eventually, as the children learn their first names, invite them to move on to playing their last names as well. This overall experience can help children process the idea of differences in sounds and uniqueness of names for each of their peers.

Scan the QR code here to observe the creation of beats using Patatap:

Or go to www.youtube.com/watch?v=KE3Qxbr0hVw.

Conclusion

Developmentally appropriate practice at its core is rooted in intentionality, moment-to-moment interactions (Copple and Bredekamp 2009). A self-selected center time can be the time to capture many of these interactions. Children enjoy music and expressing themselves through song. Teachers need to provide all sorts of ways for children to express themselves, explore their creativity, develop relationships, and refine their negotiation skills. Experiences that include an element of music and sound are perfect stages to provide children opportunities to develop these competencies.

6 Forms

6.1 Music Mixing Record Sheet

www.redleafpress.org/techpk/6-1.pdf

6.2 Xylophone Program Record Sheet

www.redleafpress.org/techpk/6-2.pdf

6.1 Music Mixing Record Sheet

Name/s:	Date:

Describe child's ability to take turns:

Describe child's ability to advocate for his or her own ideas:

Next steps for child:

6.2 Xylophone Program Record Sheet

Name/s:		Date:
Songs to be programmed (circle one):	Prewritten:	Child-written:

Program written in Wonder Workshop:

Child self-assessments after trying out program:

Describe perseverance:

Next steps for child:

Social Studies

Most children do not have memories of their time in preschool; however, I do have a few. I lived in a small town and attended a preschool in the basement of Holy Angels Church. If you were to ask my parents, they would say that I was quite the compliant child. I was not a rule breaker, or even bender; I followed them to a *T*. I was not one to push the boundaries of any kind. Being this way, I was quite intrigued, entertained, and at the same time confused when I saw other children challenge rules of the classroom or the playground. I wondered what their motives were and why they thought it was important to go against the rules.

But one day I did break the rules. I had gotten into an argument with another boy. I cannot remember exactly what we were arguing about, but I can remember how I tried to let him know that I disagreed. I bit him! I found myself very upset with the disagreement but also upset with myself at the choice I had just made. I was placed in the very popular and traditional time-out chair. After some time, one of my teachers came over to talk with me about what I had done. I had not listened to much of what she had to say before my feelings about the situation launched me into another poor choice—I kicked my teacher in the shin! After I did it, I again could not believe it. "How could I do that?" I asked myself.

One of the most significant areas of learning and growth in the early childhood years includes social-emotional development. Children learn to share how they feel, share what they want, take turns, and problem solve nonviolently. Early childhood educators realize the importance of this area of development and therefore craft a classroom community that helps children feel safe and comfortable taking risks. During the course of my incident, I had obviously been upset and frustrated. I had trouble conveying this and sharing it using a nonviolent strategy. Today teachers of young children know of more productive, developmentally appropriate strategies to help children work through social conflicts. Dan Gartrell discusses the use of a peace island in his book *The Power of Guidance: Teaching Social-Emotional Skills in Early Childhood Classrooms* (2004). In this space, children have access to a variety of tools to facilitate conversation that communicates how each child feels. After implementing one of these spaces in my classroom, I included some of these materials: puppets for role playing, cozy chairs, soft lighting for an undistracted environment, children's books on social conflicts for relevance and reliability, and a "peace wheel" to provide collaborative activities to help mend social relationships. A center like this tells students that the teacher and overall classroom community value this type of social problem solving (Mraz and Hertz 2015).

Today's technology provides classrooms with resources to help nurture the development of social-emotional skills by helping children convey feelings and connect with other people and places.

Young children do not have the cognitive capacity to feel remorse (Nelsen, Erwin, and Duffy 2007), so I included a wheel of choices comprised of six activities that children could engage in after they resolved their conflict. These activities included the following:
- play a game together
- paint a picture together
- build a block tower together
- play instruments together
- enjoy a book together
- explore the sand and water table together

Secret E-Reader

In *Teaching in the Digital Age: Smart Tools for Age 3 to Grade 3* (Puerling 2012), I spoke about how video conferencing experiences can help children develop identities as authors by having Skype conversations with authors and illustrators. As teachers invite individuals for these virtual visits, such experiences not only expand the classroom community but also help children understand that individuals can be accessible in multiple ways.

A popular classroom practice in the elementary grades is to have secret readers come to the classroom and read a story to the class. A secret reader is a person of significance to a child in the classroom, such as a parent, grand-parent, aunt, or uncle. Young children enjoy being able to speak about what is important to them: family, traditions, foods, and so on. These are popular conversations at the beginning of each school year as the children get to know each other. They learn about each other's similarities and differences, likes and dislikes. As children talk about their families, they will most certainly talk about family members who do not live with them or even near them. Teachers can use video conferencing to invite those individuals into the classroom as secret readers. Consider these possible secret e-reader individuals:

- older sibling at college

- aunt/uncle/cousin living across country

- grandparent/family member unable to travel or in assisted living

- former student who has moved away

Supporting Learning: Anytime a child's parent or family member is invited into the classroom to do something, children glow with delight. Children are naturally egocentric at this age, and teachers can use this developmental stage to help nurture growth and learning in other areas. By inviting children's relatives into the classroom to be guest readers, teachers generate interest and enthusiasm. As these guests read aloud, the children see other adults enjoying reading and seeing themselves as readers. We want young children to make connections with books and other people, and this is a meaningful way to do that.

Assessment and Documentation: After reading the story, the guest may ask the class questions about the story. The guest may ask questions related to connections the children may have to the story or the characters. As the children answer these questions, the teacher can jot down notes that may help with

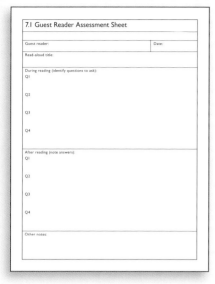

7.1 Guest Reader Assessment Sheet

Guest reader: | Date:
Read-aloud title:

During reading (identify questions to ask):
Q1

Q2

Q3

Q4

After reading (note answers):
Q1

Q2

Q3

Q4

Other notes:

a follow-up conversation about the story later. Consider using the Guest Reader Assessment Sheet (7.1) to help gather information about the children's experience and comprehension of the story.

Sharing Learning with Others: Teachers can share this experience with photographs or videos in a newsletter or e-mail to families. If using a video conference resource with secret e-readers, such as Google+, teachers can record the entire video conference and share that with families. Use what you know about your families to determine the best way to inform them of these types of classroom events. Having the ability to invite these individuals into the classroom not only strengthens the classroom community, which is the foundation for learning, but also supports the students' literacy development as they see important people sharing their love for reading.

Video Messages

Having a guest reader can free the teacher up to jot down more comprehensive notes during the experience.

As teachers begin to help children understand the many ways people can communicate using technology, the children begin to understand and consider how they can use such methods in their own lives. A student named Kate had to leave our school because she was moving away with her family. Kate was aware of some of the ways in which people can keep in touch. Being too young to write or type a letter with all the information she wanted, she decided to send a video message to Dr. Jean Robbins, PhD, our early childhood division head. Jean was ecstatic to get the video and sent a video message back to her.

Scan here to view the video sent by Kate:

Or go to www.redleafpress.org/techpk/v-1.aspx

Scan here to view the video sent by Jean:

Or go to www.redleafpress.org/techpk/v-2.aspx

In this experience, Kate was able to identify an accessible strategy that could help her carry out the task she wanted to do. She had seen videos and video conferencing at school and perhaps at home, and decided to use the strategy herself. This is an excellent example of how children in this digital age can employ technology in their own lives after seeing it used appropriately in school, at home, and elsewhere.

Supporting Learning: In this experience, Kate was able to use technology to reach out and reconnect with someone at her previous school. Young children are not able to compose full e-mails yet, so she used what she knew about technology and matched it up with what she knew she was able to do. Having this successful experience of reaching out will only encourage her to continue to use technology as adults do each day.

Assessment and Documentation: This exchange occurred outside of a classroom experience, but if her teacher were to have been involved, he would note that Kate is becoming aware of the resources around her and how she can use them to connect and reconnect with individuals. Kate has moved out of the stage of using technology only for game-like entertainment and into a stage that is using resources more intentionally.

Sharing Learning with Others: This video exchange was shared with Kate's previous teachers so they could see what Kate looks like today and see how she is doing. These video clips, though simple, say a lot and go a long way when attempting to maintain relationships.

Feelings Book/E-Book

In early childhood, young children are developing vocabulary to describe wants, express needs, and share information, including how they feel. This is particularly important because children feel a wide range of emotions, just as adults do. Adults, however, have the vocabulary to articulate how they feel. When children do not have this ability, they can easily become frustrated and upset. As teachers plan spaces and experiences in their classroom, they think about how to foster emotional language development. One possible experience could be to create a Feelings Book. This book could house photographs depicting the feelings shown in children's facial expressions. This book could be visited often and could be used for reviewing and adding new words as they come up. Consider these possible entry points to introducing new emotional vocabulary words:

- after a heated conversation between children in the class

- after reading a children's book with characters exhibiting feelings

- after seeing a play with characters exhibiting new feelings

- after a child asks a question about a certain feeling word

Here are two possible ways to assemble this book:

Printed Book

Take snapshots of children and print them out. Place photographs on pieces of paper labeled with the appropriate feeling or emotion. Laminate the pages for durability and then bind them together. This book can be used with children one-on-one or placed under a document camera and projected on a large screen for discussion.

E-Book

Use the Book Creator application to create pages with these photographs, labeled with the appropriate feeling or emotion. In this application, video and audio can also be added if the children want to add more information about that feeling. This book can be exported to the iPad's bookshelf. It can then be used with children one-on-one or hooked up to a projector to project the book on a large screen for discussion.

There are several occasions when this book will make for an important conversation tool. Here are some possible classroom events to consider using the book:

- during a social problem-solving conversation between children

- when noticing a child appears withdrawn from other children

- when reading children's books and exploring characters' feelings

- on the playground

- during a class meeting

In conjunction with the book, consider using puppets or children to act out the feelings in the book.

Supporting Learning: Emotional vocabulary, self-regulation, and empathy are difficult but important skills and concepts to obtain in early childhood. It is important that teachers provide the tools necessary for children to acquire them in a fashion that is developmentally appropriate, motivating, and non-threatening. In the process of making a book, the children explore literacy concepts while at the same time learn new emotional vocabulary that will help them effectively articulate their feelings and emotions during times of social conflict.

Assessment and Documentation: As the children choose words to add to their book, it is the teacher's hope and intention that the book will be revisited over and over again and used as a tool to support the children in their conversations around conflict. The teacher should lend a close ear when the children have these conversations to be sure that the vocabulary is being used accurately. If one child misuses a word, the other child could get confused and perhaps more upset. A teacher standing nearby can listen and offer strategies or more accurate words for the children to use if they seem to be having troubles. If many of the children are having difficulties with the words, then the teacher should plan additional experiences around those words. A teacher who notices that the words are being used accurately and effectively should consider that a green light to introduce more sophisticated words.

Sharing Learning with Others: How the book is shared depends on how it was created. If it is a printed, bound book, it would be wise to keep the original copy in the classroom. Teachers may consider making copies of the book for each child to take home. If this rich resource is at home, the child will more likely transfer the problem-solving skills learned at school into the home. Moreover, if the parents are aware of the emotional vocabulary being used at school, they can begin using the words as well to reinforce the integration of words into the child's lexicon.

As early childhood educators know, young children develop and acquire social-emotional skills at varying rates. Some children need more time and support than others and may benefit from having a book unique to them that they can use when necessary. Technology can be used in a variety of ways to differentiate the support necessary for individual children.

Establishing Relationships through Digital Pen Pals

As part of a fellowship with the Fred Rogers Center, I was the concept designer of an iPad application that brings art and communication together to make a digital pen pal interaction possible for young children. ChromaKids is an application that invites children to create a story using illustrative tools, size-adjustable stickers, and a recorded narration. These stories can then be shared with others they have connected with within the application. The receivers can then add or change the illustration, as well as add their own narration to the story.

This application was illustrated by friend and colleague Todd Parr. His books focus on identity, acceptance, and other socially relevant issues. Scan this QR code to learn more about his publications:

Or go to http://www.toddparr.com/books.html.

Supporting Learning: A significant skill and concept for young children to understand is that stories have several parts. In the simplest terms, they are composed of characters; a plot, including a problem and a resolution; and a setting. Very young children are often excited about the idea of telling stories to others. These stories are often meandering and changing by the moment to hold the listener's attention, but the power in this experience is that the child is learning that he has agency in the development of this story. ChromaKids provides children with an opportunity to explore this agency in another way. They are able to use art and an audio recording to create their story, but then invite another individual into the process of developing and changing this story. It is important for children to learn that stories can be created in all sorts of ways—by a solo author or multiple authors—and also in various mediums or venues: written down, recorded, through a poem, through art, in the car, around a campfire, or at the dinner table.

Assessment and Documentation: As parents and teachers observe children building their stories in ChromaKids, they have a documented form of their stories in both art and recorded dictation. This is a significant and authentic sample of the children's ability to demonstrate their understanding of how to integrate the parts of a story listed earlier. Individuals can also observe the following:

- how the child is able to change the story and to what degree

- how the child maintains flow

- how the child introduces new characters

- how the child experiments with action, suspense, or surprise

Sharing Learning with Others: ChromaKids features the ability to take a screenshot of the illustrated story to be saved on the iPad's Camera Roll. Beyond that, sharing is private between the users creating the story. Should children want to share their stories with their narration, they can use the photos of their illustrations saved in Camera Roll in an application such as SonicPics, Doodlecast Pro, or Educreations to create a video compiling the artwork with the narration. These videos can then be shared in a variety of ways, such as via e-mail or social media.

Scan here to learn more about ChromaKids:

Or go to https://itunes.apple.com/us/app/chromakids /id1011924921?mt=8.

Social Media to Establish Social Connections

Developing social-emotional skills does not only happen face-to-face. Children can connect and develop relationships with people in other ways while still in the classroom, in the home, on the playground, at the pool, or in the car. With the support of teachers and parents, children can utilize social media platforms to connect with experts, relatives, and other classrooms.

There are all sorts of ways to share information and connect with other classrooms, parents, and the greater community while helping children develop an idea of what it means to be a digital citizen in today's world (Davison 2013). Even in preschool and kindergarten, teachers can utilize e-mail, blogs, Twitter, and Facebook to make these connections. Friend and fellow Redleaf author Gigi Schweikert discusses the benefits of using technology to connect with parents digitally as well as face-to-face (Schweikert 2014). When technology is used, parents are more likely to read teachers' communications and respond to their requests. The information can be shared immediately and accessed with the swipe of a finger. The effort for sending this information can be less time consuming, allowing for more time spent with children. In some more traditional methods of sharing information, teachers create handouts, make copies, and put them in folders and backpacks. Sending a quick e-mail, updating a blog, or posting a tweet can take just minutes.

Teachers can create a class blog that shares news about what is happening in the classroom. Writers can include all sorts of features to make their class blog as informative and interactive as possible. Here are some of the features one might consider for a class blog:

- videos
- photographs (of children and work samples)
- audio files
- links to parent resources
- discussion boards
- book recommendations

To help children feel as though they are making connections with the readers, invite them to help identify what is to be posted on the blog. Moreover, invite them to help compose and create the actual content posted. Perhaps an audio file of two children discussing their favorite Karen Beaumont books is posted, with a comment feature that allows readers to reply to the post and engage in conversation with the children. It is in these conversations where children can feel the most significant connection. They feel proud that readers have found their ideas and information interesting enough to read and comment on.

Talking to the children about the blog and its purpose is important. For example, "We are writing this class blog because we know that your families are very interested in what is happening in our classroom. This will tell them all about it! It's like they can be in our classroom without actually being here."

To make this conversation less abstract, show them the web page and connect what is posted to the experiences they have had in the past. This will help the children recognize the significance and their ownership of the blog. Invite parents to come visit the classroom to share what it was like to visit the blog online and read about what has been happening in the classroom.

There are a variety of user-friendly resources to help teachers create and manage their blogs:

- WordPress (scan here to visit website):

 Or go to https://wordpress.org.

- Blogger (scan here to visit website):

 Or go to www.blogger.com/start.

Remember that the Voice Recorder application can be used to create these audio files to be posted on the blog.

Be sure to invite the parents to look at the blog with their child so that the child can elaborate on the events they are reading about. Also, be sure to have the children share with the class what it was like to look at the blog with their families.

- Weebly Education (scan here to visit website):

Or go to https://education.weebly.com.

Be sure to review these options and what it takes to create the blog. Each of these sites is organized a little differently so it is important to decide which way works best for those involved: teachers, teacher assistants, children, parents, and administrators.

Supporting Learning: A class blog offers classrooms a way to connect with the world that a website does not. In the process of creating a blog, young children can learn the difference between a website and a blog. The school website shares information about the school community, school-wide events, and the school calendar. A classroom blog discusses details about what is going on in a particular classroom. With the help of adults, students can post all sorts of items, as listed earlier, to help readers understand what is happening in the classroom.

Assessment and Documentation: A classroom blog can be prepared in a variety of ways. A teacher deciding to rotate classroom bloggers could learn about what each child thinks is particularly interesting to share with the readers. As the teacher and the child chat about what will be shared, the teacher will gather information about the child's perception of what a blog is intended for.

Sharing Learning with Others: The blog itself is meant to be shared. Alert families before the blog is started so that once it's up and running, an audience will already be waiting to read what is posted and will then perhaps comment back, if that's the approach the classroom chooses to take. A blog is an authentic, class-effort strategy to remain connected to families and to connect with other classrooms.

A class blog is different than a school website. A blog is updated regularly with new classroom events, celebrations, and announcements. A website is typically used to inform prospective families on the mission, vision, curriculum, staff, and location.

Reaching Out with Classroom-Based Twitter and Facebook Accounts

Twitter and Facebook have become very popular ways for individuals to connect with friends, family, and other professionals. They have also become a means for schools and classrooms to reach out and connect with people all around the world.

Twitter and Facebook are each organized in their own unique way. Spend some time in each of them to decide which platform works best for your community. If you do not have a lot of personal experience, consider sitting down with a friend or relative who uses these platforms often. They can give you a tutorial of the options and opportunities Twitter and Facebook can provide. Teachers may consider surveying their parent populations as well to determine which platform they use most. This may be helpful in making a decision.

Conversation through comments and posts is where the children will feel the greatest connection with others, so choose a platform that will make engaging in conversation easy. Consider asking yourself these questions to help you determine which platform best fits your needs:

- Who do we plan to get connected with?

- How often do we plan on posting?

- Who do we think will follow us?

- What do we plan on sharing?

- Will we be posting photographs?

- Will we be posting videos?

- How comfortable am I with using Facebook or Twitter?

The answers to these questions may help you decide which platform is best. Remember, if you later learn that the other platform turns out to be better, go ahead and switch; just be sure to alert your followers that you are switching.

Supporting Learning: Facebook and Twitter are different methods of sharing than a blog. A blog is more in-depth, whereas Facebook and Twitter are typically short comments sent out to followers. With Twitter, the children learn about some of the concepts of an audience. First, they know the number of individuals in their audience (the number of followers). They also learn that they can see what people think or have to say about their quick posts by reviewing the responses or the number of retweets.

Assessment and Documentation: As the year goes on, teachers can begin to get a sense as to whether the children are understanding the intentions and concepts of using Facebook or Twitter. For example, perhaps the class goes on a field trip to a farm, and while on the farm, they see two baby chicks hatch out of eggs. The classroom is noticeably excited, and then one of the children announces, "That was really cool. We should tweet that on Twitter!" That announcement would indicate that the class is beginning to understand the concepts behind sharing through social media.

Sharing Learning with Others: Facebook and Twitter, like the blog in the previous strategy, are intended to be used as avenues for sharing information. Classrooms should alert as many interested people as they can if they are going to engage in social media. This way the audience is set and conversation is more than likely going to happen if the classroom makes a post. The experience is more authentic if the class gets individuals responding to their posts.

Fostering Independence with QR codes

I have mentioned the use of QR codes throughout this book. They are a fairly simple way to get families in touch with the faces and voices of the classroom. A significant skill that early childhood educators must nurture is independence. Teachers build in scaffolds and routines that help children determine the best strategy to get something done on their own. High-quality early childhood centers typically have the classroom divided into learning spaces or centers. At these centers, the children usually have a specific task or a choice of activities. As children tend to do, they may forget what the tasks are or how they are to interact with the materials provided. Teachers can post QR codes to videos of the teachers providing the instructions. This way the teacher can be free to work more directly with other children without having to be interrupted.

Before putting these QR codes in centers, teachers need to be sure to introduce QR codes to the children. This introduction will look different depending on the ability and backgrounds of the children. When crafting your introduction(s), be sure to discuss these points:

- What does a QR code look like?

- Where have you seen a QR code before?

- What do we use QR codes for?

- How could we use QR codes in our classroom?

After discussing these points, introduce how the QR codes will be used in the classroom. Discuss how they will help the children remember what the classroom spaces are used for and how to use the materials in the classroom.

Supporting Learning: As students begin to utilize the QR codes to access information about the routines and materials in the classroom, they begin to learn about the many ways that children and adults can access information independently. This independence is important. If children feel they can be independent in one activity, they are more likely to attempt being independent in another. The children are also beginning to learn how technology can be used to access information. Previous strategies have mentioned using websites, social media, and video conferencing to access information. These experiences will add opportunities we have with technology.

Assessment and Documentation: As the children use the QR codes in the classroom, the teacher may begin asking the group about where else they have seen them and if they were able to scan them (with the help of an adult) to see what they were able to learn from them. In this digital age, QR codes are becoming a new environmental print. Children will begin noticing them on the sides of busses, on fast food cups, on shopping bags, and at bus stops.

Sharing Learning with Others: At a school open house, the children can lead their families on a tour of the classroom. If they forget what the role or task is at a given center, they can show their families how they scan the QR code to learn or be reminded about what their job is at that particular center. In doing so, the families will see how technology and digital media is being used intentionally to support their children's success and independence.

Conclusion

Social-emotional development is a large part of early childhood education. Teachers can use the wide range of technology tools to help support this ongoing development from printed books and e-books to social media networks. No matter what the experience is, it is important that teachers are well aware of the social-emotional state of the group and use that state as the guide for the tools they decide to use with the group, rather than choosing a tool or resource first and then finding a way to make it work

7 | Forms

7.1 Guest Reader Assessment Sheet

www.redleafpress.org/techpk/7-1.pdf

7.1 Guest Reader Assessment Sheet

Guest reader:	Date:

Read-aloud title:

During reading (identify questions to ask):

Q1

Q2

Q3

Q4

After reading (note answers):

Q1

Q2

Q3

Q4

Other notes:

Health and Safety | ⑧

I REMEMBER THE DAYS IN EARLY ELEMENTARY SCHOOL when the doctor, dentist, police officer, and firefighter would come and visit my classroom. Unfortunately, rather than listening to the important information they were sharing, I generally spent most of the visit wondering what kind of exciting token I would be taking home with me. I wondered, would it be a sticker, a badge, or a helmet? The dentist's visit was the most exciting to me. Not only was it a change from the day-to-day routine, but it was also a sure indication that I was going to get a new toothbrush. The information shared by the dentist, paired with receiving a new toothbrush, was always successful in recharging my energy and motivation to making sure I brushed my teeth an appropriate amount of times per day.

Inviting experts in these and other areas is important to help children value living a healthy lifestyle. Alternatively, putting young children in charge of being the expert to share important information is impactful as well. Today it is possible to invite experts like these into the classroom without having them step foot in one. Busy schedules can make it difficult for these individuals to take time out of their day to travel to a school for a visit. Skype, FaceTime, and Google Hangouts are easy-to-use resources to facilitate a video conference

Facilitating conversations using digital media helps children develop an understanding that mobile devices have many uses. Typically, the most common use they understand is playing games. We provide children with valuable knowledge when they see these devices being modeled for experiences such as these:

• capturing moments with videos or photos
• researching in attempting to answer a question
• communicating with others

conversation. These conversations can be had anywhere that is convenient for your guest, from a desk in the airport to a hotel room during a business trip.

Wash, Wash, Wash Your Hands! Creating a Hand-Washing Commercial

Young children are natural explorers. Early childhood educators know that young children explore best when all of their senses are activated. As this occurs, children will plunge their hands into mud, then bring their hands to their noses for a sniff, and perhaps even their mouths for a taste. When they do so, it is important that children wash their hands often to avoid taking in unwanted germs. Early childhood educators also know that young children love to share what they know. At any age or grade level, an authentic approach to assess whether a student understands particular content is to have them demonstrate it or share it in some way. Once the children have developed the understanding as to why washing hands is important, teachers can help them discover the value in sharing that information with others.

Children love to be in front of a camera, so creating a video in which children share why washing hands is important is exciting and a meaningful assessment of their understanding.

Supporting Learning: This experience invites children to share important information regarding self-care. In creating this video under the guidance and support of a teacher, children will negotiate roles, identifying who will say what and at what time. Not only will they share what they have learned about washing hands, but they will also learn about the collaborative approach when creating videos.

Assessment and Documentation: One of the best ways to demonstrate that one fully understands a skill or concept is to teach it to someone else. The process of creating and viewing the video will provide teachers with a variety of opportunities to determine and assess whether the children have a firm understanding of particular points regarding washing hands.

There are particular moments when washing hands is a healthy choice:

- before and after a meal

- after coming in from outdoors

- after touching an animal

- after handling materials that leave residue on the hands (such as mud, foods, and paint)

- before holding a newborn baby

- after using the restroom

Healthy hand washing includes the following:

- using water with soap or a hand sanitizer

- washing or scrubbing hands until they appear clean

- cleaning up one's hand-washing space

- washing hands to avoid collecting and sharing germs with others or transferring into food

Teachers can choose a couple of the above points to determine whether they feel the children fully understand the healthy choice to wash hands. The video itself should not be the final and only assessment of the children's understanding. Anecdotal notes can be taken throughout the entire process of creating the video: brainstorming and informal conversations during a morning meeting, on the playground, during a snacktime of mealtime, and during the filming.

Sharing Learning with Others: In conversations leading up to the creation of these videos, discussing the audience is important. Determining an authentic audience is key because doing so provides meaning, purpose, and motivation for the children. To determine an authentic audience, in the context of this video, pose these two questions to the children:

Videos can be captured with all sorts of devices at varying price points. Generally, the higher the price point, the higher the quality of the footage. At the higher end, Digital Single-lens Reflex cameras take high-definition video and photographs. They also have granular settings that can provide a more skilled photographer with the opportunity to get a particular desired shot in almost any setting.

- Who do you think might need to learn how to wash their hands?

- Who might need reminders about washing their hands?

The responses to these questions will help guide who this video might be made for. Here are some possible responses:

- next year's class

- our class

- other classrooms in the school/early childhood setting

- families of children in the class

- faculty/staff of the school/early childhood setting

These videos can be shared via YouTube, Vimeo, or other video-sharing resources. Once videos are uploaded to one of these sites, a link can be e-mailed or texted to the appropriate audience. Depending on the ability of the group, QR codes can be posted outside of the bathroom to serve as access to a reminder of how to appropriately wash hands.

Environmental Safety through Voice-Over Videos

Children begin to identify various ways to interact with the environment around them. They find out early on that food will drop to the floor when released from their hands while sitting in a high chair. They learn that foods have various tastes, some preferred and some not. They find that stairs can be quite intriguing as they begin moving up and down them. Later they discover that once they have learned to walk, they can also learn to run. They recognize that tricycles, bicycles, and cars can be another way to move around. As they make these discoveries, we are responsible to guide their explorations in ways that keep them safe and healthy. At Catherine Cook School, we have adopted an approach to community building that we call ROARS. It is an acronym for Respect, Ownership, Appreciation, Responsibility, and Safety. We often help our youngest learners begin to understand these concepts using videos. As they establish a basic understanding, we invite them into the process of educating other children and our greater parent and family community. One of the easiest areas to start with is safety. Some of the typical topics for videos to be created by our youngest learners include being safe in these places and times:

- on the playground

- around ice

- in the stairwells

- during a fire, tornado, hurricane, or earthquake drill

- when crossing the street

Other situations that may be important include being safe around

- power outlets or large machines,

- strangers or large groups of people, and

- pools or large bodies of water.

These videos can be captured in a variety of ways. Several of the apps referenced in previous chapters can be helpful in creating them:

- Using photographs or videos, Green Screen by Do Ink can help children virtually relocate themselves into a place with the risk at hand. The children can then narrate their understandings and choices to remain

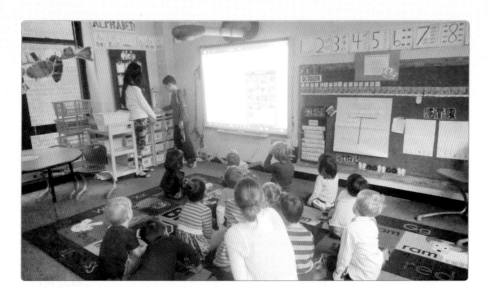

Educreations provides educators with the opportunity to create recordings like those in Doodlecast Pro. Educreations is available not only as an application but on their website.

Or go to www.educreations .com

Many early childhood settings, schools, and districts are considering the evolution of laws regarding carrying concealed weapons to determine how they address components of their curricular approaches relating to safety. I highly encourage those in early childhood settings to discuss how this new societal dynamic informs conversations and questions posed to curriculum development.

safe while they are part of the video. Learn more about how Do Ink can be used in classrooms by following them on Twitter, @DoInkTweets.

- Scan the QR code to learn more about Green Screen by Do Ink:

Or go to www.youtube.com/watch?v=ekX1mDt6QNY.

- The applications Doodlecast Pro and Educreations allow children to use illustrations or photographs of risky environments and invites them to provide an audio-recorded narration of their suggestions for safe choices.

- The application Book Creator can be used to gather all the videos created to encourage safe choices. These videos can be shared as e-books with other Apple product users or as videos with PC product users.

Supporting Learning: As children begin to explore various environments, they learn about what is safe and unsafe. As children learn these boundaries, teachers can use these videos to serve as reminders for how to operate in various situations. For example, if a preschool class is about go on a field trip to the zoo in the spring, you might replay a video made earlier in the year that underscores the importance of how to be safe in large groups or in places with lots of people. By using the children's voices in the video, teachers help young children understand that adults are not the only source for information. This experience will help children learn that their peers, videos, images, and much more can be resources for learning.

The topics of the videos they create provide children with the opportunity to revisit strategies to make safe choices in various situations. Though these videos are created in school, teachers must discuss with the children how to take these important strategies outside of school to remain safe. Consider these questions for conversations on transferring safety skills to their lives outside of school:

- You now know how to play with your friends on the playground at school. How might this be helpful when making choices at home with your brothers or sisters?

- You know that the playground will have frozen puddles in wintertime. Now that you know how to be safe around those frozen puddles at school, how might you make choices around puddles in the driveway, backyard, and sidewalks around your home?

- Walking down the stairs in a straight line is important at school. How might you walk down the stairs at a restaurant, a park, or your house when you're not in a line?

- When at school, we have practiced safety drills in case of a fire or a tornado. What choices might you make if you were at home and there was a tornado or a fire?

- When crossing the street with our class, we know that waiting for the teacher to say it is safe to cross the street is important. When you are with your family, how might you know it is safe to cross the street?

- At school only the teachers plug in and unplug anything that uses electricity, such as lamps, light tables, iPad chargers, and CD players. When you are home, what choices might you make around the items that are plugged in throughout your bedroom?

- When we go on field trips, groups stay close to the volunteers (or chaperones) for safety reasons. When you go to the park, zoo, playground, or beach with your family, how might knowing this be helpful in making choices about where you choose to play?

- On nature walks near streams, rivers, or lakes we must stay close to our groups. Why do you think staying close might be important when you are with your family on similar walks?

Assessment and Documentation: As the videos are being created, and as the students take turns doing the voice-overs, teachers have a unique opportunity to learn more about a child's ability to

- use language with media resources,

- use language and relevant vocabulary to describe a process,

- understand the sequence of particular steps or procedures,

Teachers might consider inviting children and families to capture a quick video of children following the same suggestions and guidelines when with their families. These videos can be shared informally with the rest of the class in a morning meeting or small-group center.

- articulate reasoning, and

- articulate possible consequences.

This experience provides children with the opportunity to exercise and employ a variety of cognitive skills, such as imagining and then articulating multiple-step processes; calling on prior knowledge to foresee possible outcomes given particular unsafe choices; using their definition and concept of "safe" to develop and provide solutions or alternatives to remain safe; and describing all of this using resources they may not have had much experience with before coming to school. Consider using the Safety Video Voice-Over Experience Sheet (8.1) as a way to assess a child's ability to exercise these skills.

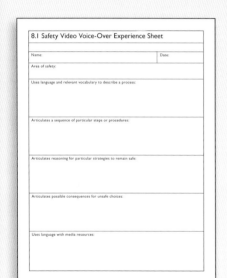

Sharing Learning with Others: These videos can be shared with various communities in a variety of ways. Consider these possible methods for sharing:

- link to video in an e-mail

- QR code in a newsletter

- classroom Facebook, Twitter, or Instagram

- classroom or school website

- school or center assembly

Sharing these videos not only allows families and other students to see what the children are learning in terms of how to interact with various environments or situations, but it also provides the children with an audience with which to share their content. If these audiences are discussed before, during, and after making the videos, the children are likely to move through the process with more motivation and excitement because preparing for an audience instills in them yet another authentic and meaningful purpose for creating the videos.

Radio Show Commercials and Podcasts

Young children come to each classroom or setting with varying levels of comfort and confidence. When children do not feel comfortable getting in front of a camera, identifying authentic ways for them to share their ideas and knowledge is important. Children are used to listening to broadcasted and streaming radio, both of which provide some sort of content via commercials or interviews between songs. Podcasts are like a radio show that is focused on a particular topic. Children can be invited to record their own radio commercials or podcasts advocating for particular practices regarding healthy living. Consider these examples for possible commercials or podcasts:

- eating nutritious vs. nonnutritious food

- brushing teeth (at school and at home)

- taking baths and washing hair (Handle this topic with cultural sensitivity as some cultures do not bathe or wash hair as often as others.)

- coughing and sneezing without spreading germs

- dealing with allergies

- wearing appropriate seasonal clothing

Radio commercials are typically quite short, less than sixty seconds. Choose this strategy if the group has not yet acquired the skills or comfort level to speak for longer periods of time on a focused topic with multiple children and with unfamiliar technology. As the year moves along with children developing language, increased comfort levels with peers, and familiarity with the classroom technology, a podcast may become a more appropriate option. If a radio commercial is the most appropriate choice for the developmental stage of the group, determining these elements is necessary:

- the big idea

- the audience

- which child will say what (consider using cues such as word or image cards)

- how the big idea will be shared

These recordings can be made with any application that records audio. Many people have had success with the free app Voice Recorder by Tapmedia. The recordings can be exported, e-mailed, and pulled into iMovie if the children choose to include images with the audio recording in a video form.

Supporting Learning: Young children are learning that content can be accessible in all sorts of ways, from people, books, e-books, magazines, newspapers, signage, social media, videos, and radio. It is important for children to understand the power of radio and the influence of the listeners. In both strategies, radio commercials and podcasts, children can experience the power of activating the ears of listeners. Knowing that they have an audience, be it other classrooms, schools, or families, they will feel a deeper motivation and interest in articulating a clearer message.

Not only will the children learn more about advocacy using radio, but they will also have the opportunity to learn from each other. Empathy is a significant skill in development at this age, so as the children brainstorm their big idea, examples, and call to action, they will be provided with the opportunity to consider other perspectives and points of view. With the help of the teacher, these perspectives and points of view can be integrated into the larger idea the group collectively chose to communicate to their audience.

Assessment and Documentation: In the recording of these radio commercials and podcasts, teachers can determine children's ability to

- pay attention to a process,

- take their turn to speak given a script, and

- speak relevantly to a given topic.

To document a child's ability to exhibit these skills, teachers can use the Radio Commercial or Podcast Experience Sheet (8.2). This sheet will help guide a teacher's recording of observations that indicate any of the above skills. Parents are always looking for a variety of work samples to illustrate their child's progress and development. The videos, along with these experience sheets, can help parents understand their child's ability to exercise these skills.

Sharing Learning with Others: As stated earlier, if the children are aware of their audience, their motivation and interest in creating these audio recordings will increase. The recordings can be shared via e-mail to provide quick access for families and others on the classroom mailing list. If the classroom web page has a wider access beyond the classroom families, the audience widens as well. Whatever method is chosen to share these recordings, sharing the skills utilized is important. Teachers often take a parent's awareness of skill sets for granted, but be explicit in what skills the children used and what skills they shared in regard to healthy living. Teachers could also include take-home questions for parents to help extend the conversation around these topics.

Using Early Graphic Design to Convey Important Classroom Messages

Young children are immersed in a world that is full of logos, imagery, and signage intended to send them particular messages. When children see the McDonald's arches, they may request a Happy Meal. When they see the neat cursive Disney logo, they may call out their favorite Disney movie characters. Teachers can harness this emerging awareness of marketing and graphic design to create signs that serve a relevant cause for the classroom. As mentioned earlier, Drawing Pad is a wonderful application to draw electronically, using a variety of mediums. In collaboration and with the support of a teacher, children can be invited to design and draw their own signage for their classroom to encourage particular practices such as these:

8.2 Radio Commercial or Podcast Experience Sheet

Name: Date:

Big idea:

Ability to pay attention to a process:

Takes turn to speak based on script:

Speaks relevantly to a given topic:

- bringing and eating healthy snacks (using images or illustrations of healthy examples, and perhaps providing those of poor choices)

- taking home cot sheets

- following the restroom use checklist

Supporting Learning: This experience helps underscore that photographs, images, and illustrations have the power to send messages. Young children can be empowered to use their familiarity with logos, marketing, and illustrations from children's books to create their own meaningful signage for a given audience, whether that be the immediate classroom, other classrooms on their floor, neighbors around their setting or school, or the families in the greater school community.

Assessment and Documentation: Early childhood educators know that children's artwork and illustrations offer a window into what they know, question, fear, and care about. There are times when children simply explore with a given art utensil, and there are times when they are extremely intentional about what they are creating or illustrating. It is up to the teacher to determine this intention, which can be done by asking the right questions:

- Can you tell me what you are drawing?

- Why is this important for you to draw?

- Who do you think should see this picture?

- Where should we post this?

- Why did you decide to draw this?

- What else could you make a sign for?

These questions can provide a teacher with a great amount of insight into the child's intention. After asking such questions, the teacher might ask children to share their illustrations and why they were created. They could then indicate where they will be posted and why. Recording these moments on video can make authentic work samples to present to families during parent-teacher conferences.

Sharing Learning with Others: The signs created can be shared in a variety of ways. When children illustrate in an application such as Drawing Pad or Doodle Buddy with the support of a teacher, they have the ability to share their electronic signs in newsletters, on social media, on the classroom website, or in text messages to families. Printed versions can be posted in the classroom or in the hallways of the school, or distributed at a school event or assembly. To provide the children with an opportunity to add a personal touch to the signs, teachers can invite children to add an illustration or short message on the back of a printed photo of the sign, which can then be sent as a postcard to a given audience.

Exploring the Human Body with Multi-Touch Mobile Technology

A variety of applications claim to provide children with the experience necessary to develop knowledge about the human body. Few, however, are as effective as Toca Doctor.

Scan the QR code to learn more about this application:

Or go to https://tocaboca.com/app/toca-doctor.

Toca Boca is an application development company rooted in child development that strives to provide age-appropriate multi-touch mobile device experiences for young children. This interactive application invites children to explore various parts of the body in accessible ways. The experience is composed of several quick games to help children understand the function and care of body parts.

Scan the QR code to take a closer look at Toca Doctor:

Or go to www.youtube.com/watch?v=yQSvWYOhlNk.

Supporting Learning: I introduced Toca Doctor to my three-year-old daughter, Lydia, and she was immediately drawn in. Not only does this application help children understand some basic anatomy, but it also helps them understand basic self-care tasks, such as brushing teeth, applying bandages to wounds, and stopping a bloody nose. Young children need concrete experiences to access what can be, at times, abstract concepts, such as health and self-care. Toca Doctor helps children access these necessary concepts in fun, meaningful, and authentic ways.

Assessment and Documentation: While engaging with children in this application, teachers can learn quite a bit about why children are making particular decisions and how they have cared for themselves in similar situations. Consider this list of questions to ask children when engaging with Toca Doctor:

- Have you ever had a scratch? What did you do to take care of it?

- Have you ever had to ask for help when you have gotten hurt?

- What have you done when you have gotten a bloody nose?

- If you saw someone with a scratch that was bleeding, what could you do for them?

- If you had a sliver or splinter, what would you do about it?

- What does your brain do for your body?

- How can you keep your brain healthy?

The discussion of these and other questions while using this application to engage with children can provide teachers with information about how a child may approach injuries or unhealthy situations. This information is helpful in planning future learning experiences related to health and wellness.

Sharing Learning with Others: Though this application has no export-able or sharable content created by the children, teachers can use an additional device to audio-record the conversation between themselves and the children. These recordings can be made with a simple audio-recording application, such as Voice Recorder by Tapmedia, mentioned earlier in this chapter. These recordings, along with a few reflection notes, can be shared with parents as work samples to exhibit a child's developing understanding of healthy living, self-care, and the basic functions of human anatomy.

Conclusion

Healthy living and safety are often left out of curriculum planning. Setting aside time to help young children understand the value and importance of self-care is crucial. A variety of developmentally appropriate experiences, both technology related and non-technology related, can help foster this founda-tional understanding. Combining the two types of experiences can provide young children with a skill set and concept foundation that helps them con-sider health and safety both at home and at school.

Forms

8.1 Safety Video Voice-Over Experience Sheet

www.redleafpress.org/techpk/8-1.pdf

8.2 Radio Commercial or Podcast Experience Sheet

www.redleafpress.org/techpk/8-2.pdf

8.1 Safety Video Voice-Over Experience Sheet

Name:	Date:

Area of safety:

Uses language and relevant vocabulary to describe a process:

working toward   successful

Comments/observations:

Articulates a sequence of particular steps or procedures:

working toward   successful

Comments/observations:

Articulates reasoning for particular strategies to remain safe:

working toward   successful

Comments/observations:

Articulates possible consequences for unsafe choices:

working toward   successful

Comments/observations:

Uses language with media resources:

uncomfortable   comfortable

Comments/observations:

8.2 Radio Commercial or Podcast Experience Sheet

Name:	Date:

Big idea:

Ability to pay attention to a process:

working toward   successful

Comments/observations:

Takes turn to speak based on script:

working toward   successful

Comments/observations:

Speaks relevantly to a given topic:

working toward   successful

Comments/observations:

Physical Education | 9

My sister April and I are just a year and a half apart in age, and my cousin Sammi is just a couple years younger than her. When we were in early elementary school, they were both members of our hometown gymnastics and dance group, the West Bend Dance Tumbling Troupe. The troupe was composed of children three to sixteen years old. Sammi joined when she was three years old, and my sister joined when she was nine. They traveled all around the state and, at times, the country. My parents, often with me in tow, followed along to see them perform. I remember being in awe of how fast the girls could move, and I envied their ability to achieve a roundoff back tuck whenever necessary. As the performances were going on, I could be found on the sidelines doing my own gymnastics. I watched my young cousin, so impressed with what she was able to do. I wished that I had discovered my interest in gymnastics earlier, and wondered if I would have been as good as she was or better.

My parents were not the only followers of the troupe. Others did as well, taking a role in the setup and takedown of the mats and speakers. Organizing these trips and events was quite a feat. The girls in the troupe were extremely hard workers. I recall my sister having four- to five-hour practices on the weekends. In any area of practice, reflection is also key. I wonder to what degree the entire team's reflections on event performances could have been enhanced if they had access to today's technology. For example, they could have played back videos of each routine, perhaps in slow motion, to look for appropriate moves, form, and spotting. These videos could have been captured with a GoPro camera clipped to each corner of the mat. An HD camera could have been set up on a tripod to capture the general audience view of the performance. These videos could also have served other purposes, including sharing with families who were not able to attend. Uploaded videos of these routines could have been stored in a YouTube or Vimeo account shared with families. They could also have been shared on a website to display the talent within the troupe.

There's no question that the best and most developmentally appropriate way for teachers to support young children's gross-motor development is to give them multiple opportunities to run, jump, climb, balance, and crawl both indoors and outdoors. Remembering that technology can be included in such experiences to enhance or support play and exploration is key.

In early childhood and school settings, time is typically built into the schedule for organized games, with the intention of developing certain large-muscle groups, sportsmanship, problem solving, and collaboration. Additionally, time should be built in for children to have opportunities for free play both indoors and outdoors to independently use and apply what they have learned about movement. Both present opportunities to include technological devices for supporting and encouraging skill development and movement exploration.

Child-Led Video Modeling

Speech-language pathologists, behavior analysts, and occupational therapists all agree that video modeling is an important consideration in nurturing children's overall development (Burdick and Biele 2014). As children become more familiar with the ways to pick up, hold, carry, and set down various technologies in the classroom, they acquire the ability to transfer that skill outside of the classroom as well. A physical education class or outdoor open play period is a great opportunity to invite young children to record or photograph each other doing various gross-motor activities as model examples for others. Consider these examples of possible gross-motor activities to capture:

- kicking

- jumping

- skipping

- crawling

- hopping

- catching

- throwing

- dancing

- galloping

- climbing

A variety of approaches can be used to encourage children to take an interest in observing, recording/photographing, and then reviewing the content. Here are a few examples of how to invite children into such an activity:

- If a classroom job board includes a classroom photographer, invite the current classroom photographer to bring a camera or multi-touch mobile device to the gross-motor play space. Provide them a few choices of which activity they would like to photograph or video-record.

- Movement Scavenger Hunt: Provide the list above in a checklist form and invite a small group to video-record or photograph as many as they can observe.

- You jump, I jump!: This requires two children. As they capture a photograph of another child doing one of the above movements, both children in the pair have to do the same movement while the other takes a photograph or video of them doing it.

To preserve the social nature of free play in large spaces, whenever possible, encourage children to conduct these activities in pairs.

- Ready, Set, SNAP!: This requires two to four children. If there are two children, each has a camera; if there are four, they split into two groups of two, with each group getting a camera. The teacher provides a shortened version of the scavenger hunt to the teams, and their mission is to be the fastest to capture video recordings or photographs of each movement on the shortened list.

Depending on the ability of the children in the group to maintain a stable hand, a short stable or rolling tripod might be helpful in supporting the young photographers in getting their shot. Additionally, depending on the devices being used, wristbands or protective cases may keep the devices safe from falling or from damage if they do fall.

Supporting Learning: The above activities provide a variety of opportunities for children to negotiate roles, take turns, use technology to record video or photographs, observe other children in gross-motor activities, and also try out various gross-motor skills. In these activities, the differentiation and practice of each gross-motor movement, rather than the technology, is the focus. The technology is present merely to provide an entry point to observation, practice, and, of course, fun.

Assessment and Documentation: As children capture videos and photographs, they are unknowingly gathering authentic evidence of a child's ability to carry out a particular gross-motor movement. These videos and photographs can be used during parent-teacher conferences to show a child's progress over time or to exhibit a particular movement that may need special attention. Some digital portfolio applications allow teachers to upload such content to an individual child's portfolio, which can be shared with families. After uploading the photos or videos, teachers can provide text or audio-recorded comments. Seesaw (https://web.seesaw.me) is a wonderful resource for such a portfolio, offering free access and use for teachers. If the setting or school has a different teacher for physical education experiences, Seesaw offers the opportunity for multiple teachers to add to one child's portfolio, streamlining assessment in a very easy way.

Sharing Learning with Others: As stated above, using a digital portfolio resource such as Seesaw is an innovative way to streamline documentation and assessment in a way that naturally offers opportunities to communicate not only with families but also between teachers. Teachers who do not have access to a digital portfolio resource can include links to these videos in a newsletter featuring particular gross-motor skills that are being focused on in the curriculum at the given time. This would be a great opportunity to help families understand what desired movements could look like at various ages, as well as offer games and strategies to help children further develop that particular movement.

Exploring Choreography

Toca Boca has developed an application called Toca Dance. In this application, children are able to choose dancers, costumes, and music, and most important, assign dance moves to the dancers. I have used this application as a way to help young learners see where they are in control of the device while engaged in a gross-motor experience. After a long musical at Catherine Cook, junior kindergarten teacher Abby Andrick wanted to engage her group in a meaningful but active experience to reset for the rest of the day. Together we used Toca Dance to facilitate a movement-based activity.

Scan the QR code here to take a look at the music video created by the class:

Or go to www.redleafpress
.org/techpk/v-3.aspx

Connecting with the Pros via Video Conference Chats

As mentioned earlier, video conferencing resources offer teachers a hurdle over some barriers for inviting classroom guests, such as funding, location, and scheduling. Video conference chats with athletes or coaches regarding safety, sportsmanship, rules of the game, inspirations, and the importance of practicing are very meaningful and authentic for young children because the guests call the children to action based on the guests' own experiences. Competition can be a difficult concept for younger children to understand. Having the opportunity to hear from and speak with experienced individuals who work in the field of physical development and athletics can be helpful.

Supporting Learning: In these conversations, children learn about the wide variety of professionals available as resources to facilitate the consideration of multiple perspectives, consequences, goals, obstacles, and inspirations. Widening their network of experts in areas that can help support learning in early childhood settings is important for teachers.

Assessment and Documentation: As these conversations are carried out, children may speak certain misconceptions, ask certain questions, or make certain conclusions. Teachers should pay close attention to what the children say to determine background knowledge, gauge self-confidence, discover misconceptions regarding physical human possibilities, and identify areas to help the overall group embrace their current abilities and feel encouraged to grow stronger in ways that are healthy and achievable.

Sharing Learning with Others: With the permission of the virtual classroom guest, these conversations can be audio- or video-recorded and shared with families in ways mentioned previously, such as e-mail, a classroom website, Vimeo, and YouTube. These videos can help families gain a firmer understanding of the various gross-motor skills in development in these early years. Physical education teachers may consider using QR codes linked to these videos on a bulletin board in the school.

Parent Game Demonstrations Videos

Malcolm Scott is the physical education teacher for the early childhood division at Catherine Cook School. He informed me that he was interested in finding a new way to show families what was happening in physical education in early childhood and to demonstrate how many of the games could be replicated and played at home. After some discussion, we decided that he would try taking short video clips of the games he was teaching the children and share them with the families through the school's Vimeo account. Since then he has been taking quick clips, under sixty seconds, that provide a clear idea of the games and concepts within as a communication strategy with the three hundred families he serves.

Supporting Learning: As families watch these videos, parents are provided a short parent education module to help further their child's gross-motor development. For children who need extra help with rules, sportsmanship, and gross-motor movement, this becomes an informal, yet very fun, homework activity that everyone is involved in. As mentioned earlier, these videos provide a window into what is happening at school in regard to gross-motor development. After viewing, parents are encouraged to reach out with questions regarding extension games and activities to support their children's development.

Assessment and Documentation: After Malcolm records these videos, he can play them back and identify children who may need help with particular movements. He can also identify whether certain rules or concepts of the game need to be adjusted, based on any indications of confusion or frustration. Alternatively, his observations may also ascertain that he needs to provide a more challenging game.

Sharing Learning with Others: From these shared videos, families are able to learn not only what games are being played but also how young children can integrate a variety of gross-motor movements into a game. As they observe developmentally appropriate activities for various ages, they may adjust any misconceptions they have about expectations regarding a child's skill ability. Physical education may not be discussed in communication with families because literacy and social-emotional development take precedence. This video-sharing approach establishes a consistent line of communication regarding skills and concepts within the physical education curriculum in preschool and kindergarten.

Conclusion

Gross-motor skills are extremely important in a child's overall development. It is imperative that teachers find intentional ways to incorporate gross-motor movement experiences in free play spaces in addition to any core physical education curriculum that exists outside of the self-contained classroom. Some argue that technology keeps children from being active. Some claim that technology has contributed to childhood obesity in the United States. These are significant concerns that need to be addressed. Early childhood educators need to consider all tools wisely and use educational technology tools thoughtfully and intentionally, in a way that is integrated into physical education that supports and encourages gross-motor movement.

Conclusion
Moving Forward

THE ACCESS POINTS TO TOOLS AND RESOURCES AVAILABLE to teachers increase every day. Social media leaves teachers feeling as if it is almost impossible to keep up with the never-ending expansion of the educational technology landscape. While the choices may seem daunting, I think it is also something to celebrate. Taking a step back, teachers now have access to all sorts of networks to research and learn about new resources. Keeping up with them all is impossible. What teachers need to do is identify a few resources that connect best with their learning style and then gradually move out from there.

Not only are the access points ever expanding, but the actual tools and resources are increasing as well. The field of early childhood education has been characterized as low-tech, but that is changing. It should change, however, in a way that keeps developmentally appropriate practice as the driver for all decisions made around the tools chosen. When I have worked with teachers in the past, I have used one phrase to help them check their intentions around their choices with educational technology tools: "If you catch yourself saying, 'Wouldn't it be cute if . . . ,' that is a red flag!" Teachers need to set aside the

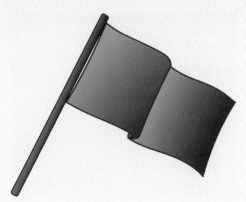

novelty and flare of the new tools and adhere to what they know best: developmentally appropriate practice.

This book is intended to provide teachers with a resource to reignite their excitement and planning in all areas of their curriculum. It is intended to help teachers expand their awareness of what young children are capable of in terms of meaningful interaction and engagement with educational technology tools.

My hope is that as you read this book, you feel capable and encouraged. Practitioners in the field must decide what technology belongs in the classroom based on what it can provide young learners. I hope that you embrace an eagerness for opportunities with the new rather than fearing the unknown. Use your intuition to make choices, and the children in your space will enjoy exceptional learning experiences.

Appendix
Mobile Device Applications

Below is a comprehensive list of the multi-touch mobile device applications mentioned throughout this book. To learn more about these specific applications, simply scan the QR code with any QR reader application and you will be taken to a link that provides more information on the details and possibilities for installation. If you do not have a QR reader application, visit one of these links to install it on your smartphone or multi-touch mobile device. QR Reader by Tapmedia is a user-friendly application with many helpful features. You can find it here:

Or go to https://itunes.apple.com/us/app/qr-reader-for-ipad/id426170776?mt=8.

Or go to https://play.google.com/store/apps/details?id=uk.tapmedia.qrreader&hl=en.

Application	iTunes	URL	Android	URL
Beatwave		https://itunes.apple.com/us/app/beatwave/id363718254?mt=8	No	Not available at this time.
Bee-Bot		https://itunes.apple.com/us/app/bee-bot/id500131639?mt=8	No	Not available at this time.
Blokify		https://itunes.apple.com/us/app/blokify-3d-printing-modeling/id705778277?mt=8		https://play.google.com/store/apps/details?id=com.blokify.app&hl=en
Book Creator		https://itunes.apple.com/us/app/book-creator-for-ipad-create/id442378070?mt=8		https://play.google.com/store/apps/details?id=net.redjumper.bookcreator&hl=en
ButtonBass Cube	No	Not available at this time.		https://play.google.com/store/search?q=buttonbass%20cube&c=apps&hl=en
ChatterPix		https://itunes.apple.com/us/app/chatterpix-by-duck-duck-moose/id734038526?mt=8	No	Not available at this time.
ChromaKids		https://itunes.apple.com/us/app/chromakids/id1011924921?mt=8	No	Not available at this time.
ComicBook!		https://itunes.apple.com/us/app/comicbook/id436114747?mt=8	No	Not available at this time.

Application	iTunes	URL	Android	URL
DJ Mix Kids Pro		https://itunes.apple.com/us /app/dj-mix-kids-pro-sound- exploration/id478653656?mt=8	No	Not available at this time.
Don't Let the Pigeon Run This App!		https://itunes.apple.com/us/app /dont-let-pigeon-run-this-app! /id459749670?mt=8	No	Not available at this time.
Doodle Buddy		https://itunes.apple.com/us /app/doodle-buddy-paint-draw- scribble/id313232441?mt=8	No	Not available at this time.
Doodlecast Pro (for iOS devices 10.0 or earlier)		https://itunes.apple.com /us/app/doodlecast-pro /id469486202?mt=8	No	Not available at this time.
Dr. PetPlay		https://itunes.apple.com/us/app /dr.-petplay-free-pretend-play /id735866884?mt=8	No	Not available at this time.
Drawing Pad		https://itunes.apple.com/us/app /drawing-pad/id358207332?mt=8		https://play.google.com/store /apps/details?id=org.pogi .DrawingPad&hl=en
Educreations Interactive Whiteboard		https://itunes.apple.com/us /app/educreations-interactive- whiteboard/id478617061?mt=8	No	Not available at this time.
Facebook		https://itunes.apple.com/us/app /facebook/id284882215?mt=8		https://play.google.com/store /apps/details?id=com.facebook .katana&hl=en

Application	iTunes	URL	Android	URL
Felt Board		https://itunes.apple.com/us/app/felt-board/id492342753?mt=8	No	Not available at this time.
Foldify		https://itunes.apple.com/us/app/foldify/id527118971?mt=8	No	Not available at this time.
Google+		https://itunes.apple.com/us/app/google-interests-communities-discovery/id447119634?mt=8		https://play.google.com/store/apps/details?id=com.google.android.apps.plus&hl=en
Google Drive		https://itunes.apple.com/us/app/google-drive-free-online-storage/id507874739?mt=8		https://play.google.com/store/apps/details?id=com.google.android.apps.docs&hl=en
Google Earth		https://itunes.apple.com/us/app/google-earth/id293622097?mt=8		https://play.google.com/store/apps/details?id=com.google.earth&hl=en
Google Hangouts		https://itunes.apple.com/us/app/hangouts/id643496868?mt=8		https://play.google.com/store/apps/details?id=com.google.android.talk&hl=en
Green Screen by Do Ink		https://itunes.apple.com/us/app/green-screen-by-do-ink/id730091131?mt=8	No	Not available at this time.
I Can Animate		https://itunes.apple.com/us/app/i-can-animate/id399760501?mt=8		https://play.google.com/store/apps/details?id=net.kudlian.icananimate2&hl=en

Application	iTunes	URL	Android	URL
iMotion HD		https://itunes.apple.com/us/app/imotion/id421365625?mt=8	No	Not available at this time.
iMovie		https://itunes.apple.com/us/app/imovie/id377298193?mt=8	No	Not available at this time.
Incredibox		https://itunes.apple.com/us/app/incredibox/id1093131935?mt=8	No	Not available at this time.
Intro to Words		https://itunes.apple.com/us/app/alpha-writer-by-montessorium/id394038232?mt=8	No	Not available at this time.
iStopMotion		https://itunes.apple.com/us/app/istopmotion-for-ipad/id484019696?mt=8	No	Not available at this time.
iTalk Recorder		https://itunes.apple.com/us/app/italk-recorder/id293673304?mt=8	No	Not available at this time.
Keezy		https://itunes.apple.com/us/app/keezy/id605855595?mt=8	No	Not available at this time.
Learning Ally Link		https://itunes.apple.com/us/app/learning-ally-link/id1131235021?mt=8		https://play.google.com/store/apps/details?id=org.learningally.LinkMobilethl=en

Application	iTunes	URL	Android	URL
Level It Books		https://itunes.apple.com /us/app/level-it-books /id584413429?mt=8		https://play.google.com /store/apps/details?id=com .ktlmobileapps.levelitbooks
Morphi		https://itunes.apple.com/us/app /morphi/id833530351?mt=8	No	Not available at this time.
Paper		https://itunes.apple.com /us/app/paper-by-fiftythree /id506003812?mt=8	No	Not available at this time.
Patatap		https://itunes.apple.com/us/app /patatap/id880626868?mt=8		https://play.google.com /store/apps/details?id=com .jonobr1.Patatap
Pinterest		https://itunes.apple.com/us/app /pinterest/id429047995?mt=8		https://play.google.com /store/apps/details?id=com .pinterest&hl=en
POP		https://itunes.apple.com/us /app/pop-prototyping-on-paper /id555647796?mt=8		https://play.google.com/store /apps/details?id=in.woomoo .pop&hl=en
Puffin Web Browser		https://itunes.apple.com/us /app/puffin-web-browser-free /id472937654?mt=8		https://play.google.com/store /apps/details?id=com.cloudmosa .puffinFree&hl=en
QR Reader		https://itunes.apple.com/us /app/qr-reader-for-iphone /id368494609?mt=8		https://play.google.com/store /apps/details?id=uk.tapmedia .qrreader&hl=en

Application	iTunes	URL	Android	URL
Quiver		https://itunes.apple.com/nz/app/quiver-3d-coloring-app/id650645305?mt=8		https://play.google.com/store/apps/details?id=com.puteko.colarmix
Seesaw		https://itunes.apple.com/us/app/seesaw-the-learning-journal/id930565184?mt=8		https://play.google.com/store/apps/details?id=seesaw.shadowpuppet.co.classroom&hl=en
Skype		https://itunes.apple.com/us/app/skype-for-ipad/id442012681?mt=8		https://play.google.com/store/apps/details?id=com.skype.raider&hl=en
SonicPics		https://itunes.apple.com/us/app/sonicpics/id345295488?mt=8	No	Not available at this time.
Spacecraft 3D		https://itunes.apple.com/us/app/spacecraft-3d/id541089908?mt=8		https://play.google.com/store/apps/details?id=gov.nasa.jpl.spacecraft3D&hl=en
Stop Motion Studio		https://itunes.apple.com/us/app/stop-motion-studio/id441651297?mt=8		https://play.google.com/store/apps/details?id=com.cateater.stopmotionstudio&hl=en
TouchCast Studio		https://itunes.apple.com/us/app/touchcast-interactive-video/id603258418?mt=8	No	Not available at this time.
Twitter		https://itunes.apple.com/us/app/twitter/id333903271?mt=8		https://play.google.com/store/apps/details?id=com.twitter.android&hl=en

Application	iTunes	URL	Android	URL
Vimeo		https://itunes.apple.com/us/app/vimeo/id425194759?mt=8		https://play.google.com/store/apps/details?id=com.vimeo.android.videoapp&hl=en
Voice Recorder (FREE)		https://itunes.apple.com/us/app/voice-recorder-free/id685310398?mt=8	No	Not available at this time.
Watee		https://itunes.apple.com/us/app/watee/id457056225?mt=8	No	Not available at this time.

References

Burdick, Carolyn, and MaryAnn Biele. 2014. "Lights, Camera, Action: Using Video Modeling." *OT Practice* 19 (14): 17–19.

Casbergue, Renee, and Dorothy Strickland. 2016. *Reading and Writing in Preschool: Teaching the Essentials*. New York: The Guilford Press.

Castek, Jill, and Laura Kretschmar. 2013. "Online Collaborative Writing Platform Drives Student Problem Solving, Critical Thinking, and Ownership of Text." *Reading Today* 31 (3): 22–23.

Copple, Carol, and Sue Bredekamp. 2009. *Developmentally Appropriate Practice in Early Childhood Programs: Serving Children from Birth through Age 8*. 3rd ed. Washington, DC: National Association for the Education of Young Children.

Cummins, Carrice. 2013. "Celebrating Teachers: Using Technology to Make a Difference." *Reading Today* 30 (5): 2–4.

Davison, Sharon E. 2013. "It's Never Too Soon to Teach Digital Citizenship." *Learning and Leading with Technology* 41 (4): 32–33.

Dinnerstein, Renee. 2016. *Choice Time: How to Deepen Learning through Inquiry and Play, PreK-2*. Portsmouth, NH: Heinemann.

Donohue, Chip. 2014. *Technology and Digital Media in the Early Years: Tools for Teaching and Learning*. Washington, D.C.: Routledge, 2015.

Gadzikowski, Ann. 2013. "Preschool and Kindergarten Classroom Strategies for the Young Scientist." In *Spotlight on Young Children: Exploring Science*, edited by Amy Shillady, 36–40. Washington, DC: National Association for the Education of Young Children.

Gartrell, Dan. 2004. *The Power of Guidance: Teaching Social-Emotional Skills in Early Childhood Classrooms*. Clifton Park, NJ: Delmar Learning.

Guernsey, Lisa, Michael Levine, Cynthia Chiong, and Maggie Severns. 2012. *Pioneering Literacy in the Digital Wild West: Empowering Parents and Educators*. The Joan Ganz Cooney Center at Sesame Workshop. Retrieved from http://www.joanganzcooneycenter.org /publication/pioneering-literacy.

IDEO. 2010. "Bringing Back the Neighborhood Pharmacy." www.ideo.com/case-study /bringing-back-the-neighborhood-pharmacy.

———. 2012. *Design Thinking for Educators*. New York: Riverdale Country School and IDEO. http://designthinkingforeducators.com/toolkit.

Isbell, Rebecca, and Sonia Akiko Yoshizawa. 2016. *Nurturing Creativity: An Essential Mindset for Young Children's Learning*. Washington, DC: National Association for the Education of Young Children.

Jackson, Robyn R. 2013. *Never Underestimate Your Teachers: Instructional Leadership for Excellence in Every Classroom*. Alexandria, VA: ASCD.

Katz-Buonincontro, Jen, and Aroutis Foster. 2013. "Integrating the Visual Arts Back into the Classroom with Mobile Applications: Teaching beyond the 'Click and View' Approach." *Journal of Digital Learning in Teacher Education* 30 (2): 52–59.

Kay, Ken, and Valerie Greenhill. 2013. *The Leader's Guide to 21st Century Education: 7 Steps for Schools and Districts*. Boston, MA: Pearson.

Kelley, Tom, and David Kelley. 2013. *Creative Confidence: Unleashing the Creative Potential within Us All*. New York, NY: Crown Business.

Lange, Michelle. 2013. "Computer Use for Poor Handwriting: When Is It Appropriate?" *Advance for Occupational Therapy Practitioners* 29 (3): 22–38.

Levin, Diane. 2013. *Beyond Remote-Controlled Childhood: Teaching Young Children in the Media Age*. Washington, DC: National Association for the Education of Young Children.

Libow Martinez, Sylvia, and Gary Stager. 2013. *Invent to Learn: Making, Tinkering, and Engineering in the Classroom*. Torrance, CA: Constructing Modern Knowledge Press.

Martinez, Sylvia Libow, Stager, Gary S. 2016. *Invent to Learn: Making, Tinkering, and Engineering in the Classroom*.

Mraz, Kristine, and Christine Hertz. 2015. *A Mindset for Learning: Teaching the Traits of Joyful, Independent Growth*. Portsmouth, NH: Heinemann.

National Association for the Education of Young Children and the Fred Rogers Center for Early Learning and Children's Media at Saint Vincent College. 2012. *Technology and Interactive Media as Tools in Early Childhood Programs Serving Children from Birth through Age 8*. Washington DC: NAEYC; Latrobe, PA: Fred Rogers Center for Early Learning and Children's Media at Saint Vincent College. http://www.naeyc.org/files/naeyc/file/positions/PS_technology_WEB2.pdf

Nelsen, Jane, Cheryl Erwin, and Roslyn Duffy. 2007. *Positive Discipline for Preschoolers: For Their Early Years—Raising Children Who Are Responsible, Respectful, and Resourceful*, 3rd ed. New York: Three Rivers Press.

Parette, Howard P., and Craig H. Blum. 2013. *Instructional Technology in Early Childhood: Teaching in the Digital Age*. Baltimore, MD: Brookes.

Puerling, Brian. 2012. *Teaching in the Digital Age: Smart Tools for Age 3 to Grade 3*. St. Paul, MN: Redleaf Press.

Scheibe, Cyndy, and Faith Rogow. 2012. *The Teacher's Guide to Media Literacy: Critical Thinking in a Multimedia World*. Thousand Oaks, CA: Corwin.

Schweikert, Gigi. 2014. "Using Technology to Communicate with Parents: Tool or Taboo?" *Exchange* 36 (3): 62–65.

Shillady, Amy, and Leah Schoenberg. Muccio. 2012. *Spotlight on Young Children and Technology*. Washington, DC: National Association for the Education of Young Children.

Simon, Fran, and Karen N. Nemeth. 2012. *Digital Decisions: Choosing the Right Technology Tools for Early Childhood Education*. Lewisville, NC: Gryphon House.

Thornburg, David D., Norma Thornburg, and Sara Armstrong. 2014. *The Invent to Learn Guide to 3D Printing in the Classroom: Recipes for Success*. N.p.: Constructing Modern Knowledge Press.

Index